5-11-62

Worship Services for Church Groups

Worship Services
for
Church Groups

�֍

by Friedrich Rest

The Christian Education Press
Philadelphia

Library of Congress Catalog Card Number 62-9088

1184086

The Lord is just in all his ways,
and kind in all his doings.
The Lord is near to all
who call upon him,
to all who call upon him
in truth.

Preface

THIS BOOK is designed for use by various church groups in periods of informal worship. Suggestions for more effective leadership in worship are stated briefly at the outset. Other sections present devotional resources for use in meetings of church officers, women's groups, men's groups, church school teachers, children, youth, families, and community groups; a treasury of devotional aids including calls to worship, scripture readings, hymns, and prayers; resource material for periods of worship marking major days and seasons of the church year; and devotional aids for special days such as Universal Bible Sunday, Reformation Day, Youth Day, and World-wide Communion Sunday.

The purpose of the book is to provide appropriate and practical devotional aids that worship leaders can use quickly and easily on numerous occasions throughout the year. The table of contents and a topical index will help in locating devotional aids for a particular theme, for a special occasion, or for use with a specific church group. The numbers given in the index refer to the numbers in front of each prayer.

The prayers are numbered and titled for easy reference. When copies of the book are available to members for unison or responsive use, the worship leader can announce the devotional aids to be used by number and title.

The number given in parentheses at the end of each prayer indicates its source. By turning to the section titled Sources, the reader may identify the origin of any prayer. Where abridgments of previously published prayers are used, that has been indicated by adding *ab* to the number in parentheses; adaptations of previously published prayers are indicated by adding *ad* to the source number in parentheses.

A selection of classical worship aids has been augmented freely by the contributions of contemporary churchmen. The local leader of worship may actually feel therefore that ministers, religious educators, and church executives have all helped him in one of his most significant Christian undertakings, that of leading in the worship of God.

To the end that many parish organizations and auxiliaries may be led in more meaningful worship at their meetings, this book is earnestly dedicated.

FRIEDRICH REST

Contents

Worship Services for Church Groups

1
Why We Worship

WHEN I was a pastor in Ohio I learned anew that people worship God for a number of reasons. I was not fully aware of the large variety of motives until the religion editor of the *Dayton Daily News* asked a Roman Catholic priest, a Jewish rabbi, and me to judge a contest on "Why I Go to Church." Ninety-one persons ranging from a fifteen-year-old high school pupil to a university professor, wrote letters. They represented religious groups ranging from a highly ritualistic body like the Roman Catholic Church to the informal Church of God.

As the three of us tried to judge the letters, we often found ourselves thinking, "If we could put the last paragraph of one letter with the first paragraph of another, what a wonderful essay we would have!"

Following the contest the essays were reviewed. The motives for going to church were listed and finally grouped under nine headings. Leaders of worship and devotion may find enlightening the following reasons why people go to church:

1. *They go to adore and thank God.* One writer said, "God made me, gave me life, a soul, parents, everything I possess. Every hour, every minute, every second depends upon the goodness and generosity of God. Why, then, can't I spend a few of those precious seconds, minutes, and hours in the church, his home?" Letters showed that worshipers wish to thank God for all he has given.

2. *They go for spiritual nourishment and strength.* Nineteen letters contained the conviction that regular attendance is nourishment for the spiritual life. The climax of this thought appeared in a quota-

1

tion emphasized by Jesus at the time of his temptation: "Man shall not live by bread alone, but by every word that proceeds from the mouth of God" (Matt. 4:4b).

In various ways people said they find new strength in going to church. Inspiring sermons give courage for the tasks of the week. Salvation—defined in one letter as humility, freedom from worries, love for neighbor, and determination to see problems through—comes through a renewal of faith in God. At church, worshipers discover the power to be what God wants them to be. All these and other expressions of divine help enable people to meet the trials they face. "The day of rest preserves the dignity of man in a day that is breaking into a faster and more demanding tempo," wrote a married woman.

3. *They go for peace and security.* Typical of the thought of a vast number of people who find comfort in church attendance was this remark: "God will hear everyone's troubles—no matter what his color or creed." God's still, small voice seems to make all things right. Comfort and an inner sense of peace come in the holy sanctuary, where God is closer than anywhere else. He alone gives peace when the world has none to offer. "I go as a sinner, he takes me in; as a lover, he loves me; in sorrow, he comforts me," concluded one person.

Only nine statements appeared containing a specific reference to forgiveness. One person confessed, "I fall on bended knee to ask forgiveness for many sins, offenses, and negligences."

Three expressed the desire for escape as one of the main blessings. In church they find a refuge from cares, where they forget the worries and sorrows of the outside world. A fourth person added, "I come out feeling like starting anew."

4. *They go for light on life's way.* Another large group of people go to church to learn. They want to learn how to understand the Bible, how to gain eternal life, how to pray for others and themselves, how to be obedient, and how to resist temptation. They yearn to have a better understanding of God, finding the church a school for the intellect, hand, and heart.

Eleven people said they look for guidance, guidance for their jobs, life, and everyday associations with people. "Sometimes in church," one wrote, "my perspective becomes clearer."

5. *They go to fulfill an obligation.* A high school boy started his essay by referring to a conversation he overheard outside his church, in which one man said to another, "Well, let's go in and get it over with." He contrasted this statement with a more joyful sense of duty. Another spoke of the church-going habit when he said, "Regularly my grandfather took me to church. The habit is a real and compelling reason." "I must go," stated another contestant simply. Still another reasoned strongly, "We ought not expect God to help us all week and not take time to go to his house of worship."

Biblical injunctions stimulating our consciences were quoted as follows: "Let us hold fast . . . not neglecting to meet together, as is the habit of some" . . . "Remember the sabbath day, to keep it holy" . . . "Could you not watch one hour?"

Ten people mentioned the power of example. God rested on the sabbath, they reasoned; Jesus was accustomed to go to church; parents set a good example; a mother of five children said, "I want to be the right kind of influence to my five children." Another mother explained, "I want my children to have the same rich heritage which is mine, a deep reverence for God and a vital interest in things eternal."

6. *They go for spiritual enjoyment.* Many are drawn to church because of the atmosphere which they find there. "The beauty of surroundings gives me peace; Sunday isn't complete unless I attend church." The quiet atmosphere is impressive to many. "I can pray more fully in church than at home, where the noise in the house disturbs my attempts to have a silent conversation with my heavenly Father," disclosed one essayist. The singing of hymns is an important motivation, judging by the frequency with which it was mentioned. "If we didn't go to church for anything else than to sing out our praise, we would be doing a good thing," wrote one who loves her hymnal. Hymns and music lift the worshiper into higher realms of thought.

One person wrote of his primary reason for going to church in this way: "All my reasons spring from one fountain, my love for

God." God knows we love him when we attend church. "When we love a person," reasoned another contestant, "we experience the urge to visit him frequently."

7. *They go to meet with others.* One person wrote, "I worship where my parents did, where my sisters and their families do now." Fellowship is desired. Several expressed the thought that the best people in any community are found in the church and they want to associate with them. Perhaps one of the most beautiful lines written by any contestant was this: "I love the music and harmony of kindred spirits as with others I join in singing praises to our Lord and Master." This sentence was written by the third-place winner, and the possibility that she may have unconsciously adapted it from Emerson doesn't detract from its beauty. The note of world-wide fellowship of the church was stressed by the essayist who stated that she wanted to share in the prayers of communicants all over the world. A few people stressed the equality of worshipers. "Church is the only place on earth where every man can feel equal to his neighbor and his brother."

8. *They go to make our world better.* Possibly the finest expression of the desire to make our world better was expressed in the essay which took first place, written by a seventeen-year-old girl.

"The chaotic situation of the world today should be enough incentive for anyone to go to church," she wrote. "I go to church because I want to do all I can to make the kind of world I will want for my children. I want a world in which they and their children can grow up without fear. I can't go to the United Nations conference and help a lot of men talk about how the world should be run, but I can do something that will have more effect on present deplorable conditions, and that is to pray. Men can never bring about anything without the help of God. If ever we need his help, now is the time."

Eighteen others felt that by going to church they were making a contribution to the cause of good in the struggle against evil.

9. *They go for a final reward.* Sixteen essays included a thought about a final reward. Most of these essayists hoped that the peace and security which they find in going to church would be theirs forever, since church-going is only a means to an end. The end is the

interesting, real, and attractive house with many mansions to which our Lord alluded. One person stated her hope for a final reward by referring to the coming of the Lord on earth.

I wish that a new sense of the majesty of God as well as his love might dwell in the hearts of men. Then the motive for worship would be ever present. The hymns we would then sing, the scriptures we would then read, the sermons and talks we would then give and hear, and the prayers we would then offer would result in deeper dedication and more wholehearted service.

Let the duty and privilege of worship permeate every Christian's heart.

O magnify the Lord with me,
and let us exalt his name together!

2

Suggestions for Worship Leaders

THE QUESTION may be fairly raised, How can we "ascribe to the Lord the glory due his name"? A feeling of inadequacy comes upon many of us when we think of how we are to give glory and honor in worship and devotion.

A hymn writer felt this problem when he wrote:

> Come, thou almighty King,
> Help us thy name to sing,
> Help us to praise.

Another wrote:

> O for a thousand tongues to sing
> My great Redeemer's praise.

One who surveyed the wondrous cross responded:

> Were the whole realm of nature mine,
> That were a present far too small;
> Love so amazing, so divine,
> Demands my soul, my life, my all.

We see in the symbolism of the vine and the branches a corporate relationship which does not permit trifling with spiritual responsibilities. There is hardly anything we can do well enough to give God the glory that is really due his name, but a satisfaction comes from believing that there was one sacrifice, one offering, one perfect self-giving to God, which is found in Jesus Christ on the cross. The sacrifice of Christ is accepted by God because the Son was able

6

to present himself a perfect sacrifice, without spot or blemish; our worship is acceptable because God loves us and therefore welcomes our sincere attempts to give the best that we have.

Four Outlines of Devotional Services

ARE there outlines of worship which have been found to be more successful than others, or do we simply put one thing after another in the hope that the result will be satisfactory?

To help arrive at a natural pattern of worship, think of yourself as you go into the church. You go expecting to meet someone more important than the Governor of your state or even the President of the United States. You are prepared to adore and praise almighty God. The setting in the church, the demeanor of the ushers, the preparation of the leaders of worship, and the worship aids themselves help you express your thoughts and feelings. After your exaltation of the holy and eternal God, you are perhaps moved to confess your inadequacy and unworthiness, following which you wish to learn from his Word. Then you are ready to hear the challenge of your faith or receive God's comfort. Next you offer your prayers of thanksgiving, intercession, and petition along with your gifts of substance as expressions of your willingness to sacrifice for him who gave so much for us. You are given a final blessing before you leave to serve. A pattern similar to this is what you will usually seek to develop. Below are four outlines that embody such a pattern.

1. The first outline is one used in a junior high school department, given in full detail in Paul H. Vieth's *The Church School*, The Christian Education Press, 1957, pages 123-125. It consists of the following:

Lighting of the Candles
Responsive Call to Worship
Unison Prayer of Invocation

Prayer of Intercession
Lord's Prayer
Hymn
The Word of God (Old and New Testament Lessons and Meditation)
The Morning Offering (Doxology and Prayer of Dedication)
Responsive Reading
Hymn
Unison Benediction

2. A service included in three annual issues of the *Youth Fellowship Kit* published by the Westminster Press was worked out carefully around the following outline:

Hymn
Opening Sentences
Call to Confession
Confession of Sins
Lesson from Holy Scripture
Hymn
Apostles' Creed
Response and the Lord's Prayer
Prayers
Silent Prayer
Closing Prayer
Benediction

In the published form of this service there were three places where material was used responsively, and four places where prayers and the creed were said in unison. The framework of this service will be found incorporated in some of the services in this book. Where the presentation of a topic is to be included, it could come before the Apostles' Creed or after the Lord's Prayer.

3. The third outline is one that was developed for the senior high department of a church school where about twenty to twenty-five minutes are used before or after the lesson period. The parts of this outline are:

Prelude
Opening Sentences or Call to Worship
Hymn of Praise or Hymn of Adoration

Scripture Reading
Prayer
Prayer Response
Hymn
Announcements
Offertory and Offertory Response
Hymn

4. When a brief service is desired, the sequence of Hymn, Scripture, and Prayer may be used. If time permits, another hymn may be inserted before the prayer. Poems, talks, readings, or recordings may be used, even in a brief service.

General Suggestions for Leaders of Worship

1. Prepare reverently and carefully with creative imagination, using simple but meaningful words. Keep in mind the reasons for worship.

2. Read distinctly and talk loudly enough so those farthest back can hear. Read the material aloud beforehand so that it is familiar. Avoid a sanctimonious tone.

3. A vital, smooth, orderly, appropriate, and progressive program is the goal to aim at in your planning. Think over the details in advance. Synchronize the parts of your program around a theme such as the home or peace, or around a special day such as Easter or Thanksgiving. Plan to move toward a climax of dedication, proceeding from adoration and praise to confession, then on to illumination, petition, and dedication. On Easter and Thanksgiving, your service may return to the expression of praise and thanksgiving as a climactic summary.

4. Notify in advance those individuals who are needed as leaders in the service. All such participants should sit close to the front and to the center.

5. Maintain a spirit of sincere reverence throughout the service.

6. Secure as much group participation in worship as is possible without violating the spirit of worship.

7. Church school worship never should be thought of as a substitute for worship in regular church services.

8. Maintain an acceptable balance between the new and the old.

Suggestions Relating to Music

1. Movement from the first hymn, usually one of adoration, to a hymn expressing quiet fellowship with God, to a final hymn carrying out the theme or challenge is desirable. Starting with a hymn of consecration is a poor way to begin a devotional service.

2. Contact the pianist or organist in advance. A prelude or a hymn stanza will help to secure a quiet atmosphere for your meeting. Special numbers should be thought of not as performances but as acts of worship.

3. Remember that a church school may learn new suitable hymns occasionally. It is a school. Part of an assembly period may be used for instruction, to be followed by a brief worship service without additional instructions or exhortations to worship. If the pianist and at least one church school group are acquainted in advance with the new hymn, the entire church school will learn it quicker. In fellowship groups other than the church school, it may not be advisable to use more than five or six unfamiliar hymns in one year. The minimum introduction of a new hymn would be the playing of it by the pianist while all are listening to the melody. Sometimes a more effective method may be used.

4. Read the words of the stanzas over before omitting any. In some hymns there is a continuity of thought which is violated if a stanza is omitted. For example, all the stanzas of "Come, Thou Almighty King" should be sung rather than just some of them.

5. Special music helps make a program successful, but advance preparation is always necessary.

6. The word "hymn" is preferred to "song," and "stanza" to "verse."

�֍

Additional Suggestions for Effective Devotions

1. It is especially important to have at least one scripture reading in nearly every devotional or worship service. When the Psalms are used, they may be read responsively from the worship section of the hymnal. A responsive service in which the leader reads a few verses of scripture and the group sings alternately may be used.

2. Prayer is one of the main elements in the devotional life. Written prayers may be altered or supplemented according to local needs. The group reading of prayers, either in unison or responsively, is often quite effective, especially if the prayers have short phrases or sentences. Wherever long and involved sentences or unfamiliar words occur, it is best for the leader to read it by himself and if necessary to rewrite parts of it so he can read it effectively. It is better not to ask the people to "repeat" a prayer, but to unite in offering the prayer.

3. If you want everyone to sing an offertory response such as "We Give Thee But Thine Own" or "All Things Come of Thee, O Lord," announce that fact before the offertory. Have the pianist play while the ushers are receiving the offering.

4. If the group is familiar with prayer responses, the use of them will be well worth considering. Announcement of a response may be made before the prayer is offered. Fellowship groups that meet at night as well as the groups that meet Sunday mornings during the church school hour usually know several responses from which a selection may be made.

5. From daily devotions, sermons, religious books, and religious

magazines, outstanding readings may be collected that will enhance
your devotional services. Popular magazines often carry significant
articles that can be excerpted or adapted if they are too long to be
read in their entirety. A summary in your own words with a quota-
tion or two may prove effective. Of all the parts in a devotional program, the talk is the hardest to keep within time limits. Usually this
is due to the desire to cover a large subject. The first step, then, is
to limit the subject. If the general subject is prayer, the subject may
be limited to one aspect of it, such as the importance of prayer or
the beauty of public prayers or the power of prayer. Even then the
time element needs to be considered. Perhaps even a smaller sub-
division of the topic can be chosen, such as the importance of regular personal prayer or the comprehensiveness of the Lord's Prayer.

6. Acquaintance with the contents and index of this book may
help you add variety and vitality to your worship services. A junior
high youth fellowship may find more than one occasion to turn to
the treasury of worship aids, to one of the special days, or to a portion of the church year. Older individuals may wish to create something new or adapt something old. It is hoped that all groups will
give prayerful preparation to the task of leading others in the worship of God, and thus help to make many meetings more meaningful
and significant.

7. Evaluate the materials to be used, to determine if they really
aid people to worship, to understand, and to express their highest
desires.

Guides for evaluation may be found in William Leach's *Handbook
of Church Management*, Prentice-Hall, Inc., 1958, pages 273-277, as
derived from P. Henry Lotz; and in Paul H. Vieth's *The Church
School*, The Christian Education Press, 1957, pages 115 and 131-132,
as derived from I. G. Paulsen.

3
Devotional Aids for Church Groups

✳

Children

1   For Children of the Parish
Blessed Lord Jesus, who hast taught us that we must be as the little
children in order to enter thy kingdom, and who didst love and bless
them most tenderly: Grant that our children may be drawn unto
thee by thy spirit and ever kept in thy service, so that walking in thy
way, they may ever show forth thy praise and be one with us in the
confession of thy holy name; who livest and reignest with the Father
and the Holy Spirit, ever one God, world without end. Amen.   (24)

2   An Adult's Prayer for Children
We beseech thee, O Father, to let thy blessing rest upon the boys and
girls of our homes. Shield them from harm. Satisfy them with all
needed good. Grant that the unfolding years may bring them strength
of character and beauty of spirit. We ask in the name of him who
increased in wisdom and stature and in favor with thee and man.
Amen.   (37)

3   A Child's Prayer for the Homeless
O God, help the people who do not have homes. Give them strength
to go along life's pathway. In the name of him who died on the cross,
we pray.   Amen.   (106)

4   In the Morning

> Heavenly Father, hear my prayer;
> Day and night I'm in thy care.
> Look upon me from above,
> Bless the home I dearly love.
> Bless all those with whom I play;
> Make me better every day.   Amen.   (28)

5   An Offertory Thought

> The needs are great:
> Our gifts are small.
> But when we share;
> There's enough for all.   (39)

6   A Personal Prayer

> Help me, God, that I may see
>   Those who need love and help from me:
> Those who are lonely, tired, or sad,
>   All those whom I may help make glad.
> Help me, God, that I may see
>   Those who need love and help from me.   (122)

7   Love and Prayer

> He prayeth best who loveth best
>   All things both great and small;
> For the dear God who loveth us,
>   He made and loveth all.   (23)

8   Ralph Waldo Emerson's Litany

> For mother-love and father-care,
> *Father, we thank thee.*
> For brothers strong and sisters fair,
> *Father, we thank thee.*
> For love at home and here each day,
> For guidance lest we go astray,
> *Father in heaven, we thank thee.*

9   **A Junior Looks at Creation**

Dear God, thy great wonders surround me: beautiful trees, lovely songbirds, the mountains so blue and so far away, the sky so full of cloud pictures, my mother and father, my sister and brothers. With all my heart I thank thee.   Amen.   (7)

Youth or Adults

10   **Stir Our Minds**

Dear Father, we thank thee for being present where two or three are gathered together in thy name, and we thank thee for being in our midst this morning. Stir our minds and our wills, so that we may eagerly learn thy will, and so that we may be ready to work and to serve as thou wouldst have us do. Forgive us when we are indifferent or neglectful, often giving excuses when we should be up and doing thy work. Enlarge our vision so that we may look beyond the present and be willing to dare for Christ and to live for him in all that we say and do. We ask this for Jesus' sake.   Amen.   (98)

11   **Guide and Lead Us**

Dear God and Father, we thank thee for our church where we may come to learn, to worship, and to serve. We thank thee for Jesus, who not only said "Go . . . teach," but also "Come . . . learn." Forgive us when we have failed to heed the invitation to learn thy will. May thy Holy Spirit radiate in us and through us so that we may witness for thee wherever we are. Bless all who teach and minister to children, youth, and adults. Create in us a desire to grow. May the living Christ guide us and lead us. We ask this in Jesus' name.   Amen.

(98)

12   **For Our Church School**

Blessed Lord, who hast given unto us the light of thy holy word, help us this day in our endeavors to learn thy truth, and to do thy will.

Give thy blessing to the classes to which we belong, and to all the members of the church school, and make us happy in thy love and favor. May we all remember what we are taught on this holy day, and have grace to improve the privileges we enjoy, to the honor and praise of thy name and the salvation of our souls; through Jesus Christ our Lord.   Amen.   (65)

13   We Thank Thee for All Thy Lovely Gifts

Heavenly Father, help us to pause now and think of thy lovely gifts to us. For the beautiful world in which we live, we praise thee. For the wonderful land in which we dwell, we thank thee. For the Christian homes from which we come, we bless thee. Teach us how to thank thee through our gifts to others who have little. Make us willing to do without things we really want that others may have the things they need. In the practice of doing this, may we find such joy as Jesus knew when he gave himself for us and went about doing good.   Amen.   (2)

14   God Cares

I need not wait for special times
To speak to God in prayer,
Nor do I always have to kneel
To feel that he is there.
No matter what the time or place,
I only need to see
That God with all his perfect love
Is here to care for me.   (75)

15   For Young People's Groups

O loving God and Father, who givest us richly all things to enjoy, help us to live in the world and to enjoy the world without being lost in its richness. Help us to use the things of this world as a trust from thee. To that good end, keep us ever in thy presence, that the glory of the eternal may shine in the beauty of the temporal. We pray through Jesus Christ, thy Son, our Lord.   Amen.   (44)

Women's Groups

16   A Meditation-Prayer for World Fellowship

Our Father who art in heaven,

Hallowed be thy name,

Thy kingdom come—to all the world, our Father, may thy kingdom come, not to a fortunate few who by reasons of birth or accident today are thrice blessed, not only to us in this country who have so many blessings, but to all those others—in far off lands, children of thine also, who have suffered so long and so much and who have paid so dearly the price of life. May thy kingdom come to all the world—thy kingdom—the true brotherhood of man everywhere, when each of us shall realize deeply and fully his responsibility to others, the responsibility of sharing our sorrows, our burdens, and our joys.

Thy will be done on earth as it is in heaven—thy will that to serve thee best we must serve our fellow man, realizing humbly the words, "As you did it to one of the least of these my brethren, you did it to me."

Give us this day our daily bread—not only for our bodies but for our spirit's strength. May we see with our hearts those countless thousands of our brothers to whom the quest for daily bread is a grim struggle. Give us the bread of compassion that we may share with others whose hunger of the body matches their hunger of the spirit.

And forgive us our debts—the debt we owe to thee for the gift of life and its blessings; the debt we owe to others who are also thine own; the debts we can never pay to those who have borne the brunt of war's sufferings that we might live in peace and prosperity; the debts of omission, the words we could have spoken, the burdens we could have shared, tragedies we could have softened by showing that we care. Forgive us for our debts as we forgive our debtors.

Lead us not into temptation—the temptation of taking the easy road of indifference to the needs of our fellow human beings, the temptation to say that as long as we are safe and comfortable we will leave well enough alone. For we realize that it is never well enough with thee whenever one of thy children is in need.

And deliver us from evil—the evil of a thankless heart.

May we come to see with our inner hearts the greatness and richness of thy gifts to us. May we in our gratitude for so much, share with those who have nothing but the will to survive. May we realize it is a privilege to share with those who are struggling against want and need and fear in devastated lands, who are working today against such great odds. May we help to keep alive the fellowship of human beings everywhere and so reach the warmth and light of true brotherhood of man in one world under God.

For thine is the kingdom, the power, and the glory forever and ever.   Amen.   (83)

17   For a Women's Conference

Dear Father of us all, we have gathered here for the enriching days before us as delegates, visitors, wives; as presidents, staff, and board members; but especially as earnest, seeking women.

Take us—change us—use us.

Bring us to a sharper awareness—to a fuller expression of churchmanship. Help us to grow in Christian womanliness.

When arrogant and proud of opinions held, humble us. When timid and self-centered, release us through thy selflessness.

Channel our judgment and our decisions through thy wisdom and thy love. Help us to reflect not only thy tenderness and thy serenity —help us to reflect thy courage also.

Heavenly Father, take us—change us—use us.   Amen.   (81)

18   For a Women's Conference

We thank thee, our Father, that thou dost know the deep need of our lives. Thou hast led us here into green pastures and beside still waters. We thank thee that in quietness we may lift our spirits to thine and rest in thee above our problems and the world's confusion.

We thank thee for those who have arranged this conference, and for our leaders and teachers. Pour upon them thy Holy Spirit, that he may bring refreshing strength through them to each one here. May we not leave this place until we are renewed in body and mind, giving ourselves fully to hallowing thy name, to the coming of thy kingdom, and to the doing of thy will. In Jesus' name, we pray. Amen. (107)

19 Guide and Direct Us

O God, who art the Creator of the universe, the Preserver and Redeemer of all mankind, we thank thee for the majesty and greatness of thy wondrous works, especially for revealing to us thy ways, thy truth, and thy will in Jesus of Nazareth.

As we are gathered here in fellowship, we ask thee to bless this organization. We pray thee to guide and direct us that in turn we may be a blessing to others. For our Master's sake, we pray. Amen. (102)

20 For the Spiritual Life of the Women of Our Church

Our Father and our God, we lift our hearts in gratitude to thee for the opportunity and challenge of life, for the realization that thou hast placed us here for thy honor and glory and for intimate fellowship with thee now and in the life to come.

We thank thee for the stirring within us that draws us steadily to thee. Do thou, our Father, so pour thy spirit upon every woman in the church, that each one may feel herself a vital part of thy divine plan. Lead us daily to a time of holy silence where mind and soul and body find their harmony in thee. Kindle us with the flame of thy love; give us hearts to know thy truth and wills to become selfless channels of thy life. We pray in Jesus' name. Amen. (107)

21 Use Us

Dear Father, we worship and adore thee. We thank thee that we may enter thy presence and commune with thee, our Creator and our God. We are grateful that thou hast made us in such a way, that even while hands are working at common tasks and minds are busy, our hearts may still rest in thee.

Teach us to lift our eyes to the hills from whence our help comes, to abide in thee always as branches remain in the vine. Forgive us for everything in our hearts which keeps thee from entering. Give us a simple childlike faith, and teach us how to pray. Stir us to intercede for others, so that alone and in groups we may open our lives to the inflow of thy love. Use us to send thy healing light into all areas of the world's need. In Jesus' name, we pray.   Amen.   (107)

22   Gratitude for Women's Work
Dear Lord, we give thee thanks for the place that women have had in the friendship and kingdom work of Christ, their ministry in the early church, and their labors through the centuries. We are grateful for all that the women of this church mean in so many avenues of service. In the noble tradition of Mary and Martha, Dorcas, Lois, and the women of Berea, may they work effectively to strengthen this church and extend thy kingdom of love, mercy, and spiritual light. We pray in the name of Jesus Christ our Lord.   Amen.   (33)

23   For the Start of a Women's Board Meeting
Our Father, who hast promised to be with us always and who hast graciously fulfilled that promise in the coming of the Holy Spirit, guide us, we pray, in the work of our executive board, that we may never be content with merely forming an organization or planning a program. Help us to open our lives to thy great power, that our planning shall be a means to spirit-filled lives among the women of our church, lives radiant with thy life and love.   Amen.   (5)

24   For the Beginning of Any Meeting
Gracious God, we come humbly to thee at the beginning of our meeting. We would come expecting to meet thee, knowing that thou dost reward the reverent worshiper with thy presence; we would come with open minds, knowing that thou wilt enlighten us with thy truth; we would come eager to serve, knowing that thou dost desire to use each of us in ministries of love for others.   Amen. (6)

25   For a Women's Meeting

O Lord, we pray thy blessing upon the women of our church. Thou who are perfect beauty, truth, and goodness, touch the lives of our women that each may be a reflection of thy beauty, a revelation of thy truth, and a channel of thy goodness. Grant us to be winsome Christians seeking always to place thy things first in our lives and to help our families and neighbors to do likewise; for Jesus' sake. Amen.   (5)

26   For a New Dedication

Father of time and space and life itself,
God of every hour's need and every day's demand,
Maker of men and Lord of life,
Once more we come to thee in praise and prayer.
Like men of old we live in an age of change into the unknown.
Again the difficulties of the human family seem too great for us.
Again our failures loom larger than our virtues.
How shall we meet this day?
How shall we rise when our weakness overtakes us and our problems overwhelm us?
How shall we witness with radiance and joy?
O Lord Jesus Christ, Revealer of God, move through us.
We know that we are not alone; we know that we are upheld and highly authorized;
We know whom we have believed.
We affirm his holy presence and divine direction in every day and in all decisions.
Help us, we beseech thee, in this new dedication.
Cleanse us of our pride and complacency, renew us in our purpose to obey,
Redeem us through thy mercy and use us that with clear and certain voice
We may speak and live thy good news to men and give courage to all who need it.

In the spirit of our Lord Jesus Christ, we offer our praise and
our petitions,

Now and forever more.   Amen.   (146)

27   For Missionary Work

Our heavenly Father, we come to thee with thanksgiving for the
manifold tokens of thy loving-kindness and tender mercy which thou
hast given us. We bless thee for our share in the great mission committed to thy church. We rejoice in the vision of the harvest ready
throughout the world, in the laborers who have heard thy call and
have devoted themselves to thy service, and in all that thou hast
enabled us to accomplish. Fit and prepare us, we beseech thee, for
our high calling. Help us to open our hearts unto thee, that thou
mayest dwell within us. And do thou cleanse us from every sin and
stain, that we may serve thee with pure hearts fervently; through
Jesus Christ our Lord.

We pray thee, O gracious God, that thou wouldst give thy blessing
to us as a missionary society. Prosper us in every work already under-
taken, and enable us by thy grace to enlarge our purposes and extend
our efforts. We spread before thee our hearts' desire and our plans,
seeking thy counsel and thy strength. Help us to go forward trusting
in thee. We commend to thy fatherly care those who labor in our
behalf, whether in our own country or regions beyond. Sustain them,
we beseech thee, in health of body and comfort of mind. Cheer their
hearts with thine own presence, and fulfill in them thy joy. Inspire
others to offer themselves for a like service, that there may ever be
laborers in thy harvest.

O merciful Father, bless all the works of mercy in which we as a
society are engaged. We remember before thee the hearts that are
hungering for thee; the aged that are bowed down with weariness
or sorrow; the men and women sorely pressed by the struggle of life;
and the children in need. Help us to love them, even as thou hast
loved us, that we may minister to them in the name of Jesus Christ
our Lord.

O divine Helper, we entreat thee, put into the heart of every woman and child deep thankfulness for thy manifold goodness to them and a faithful purpose to offer unto thee the utmost they can give, that our treasury may be filled and thy needy ones may be cheered and refreshed. Guide us in the use of the resources entrusted to us. Bless us in our fellowship as laborers together with thee. May thy name be glorified in the service we render; through our Lord Jesus Christ.   Amen.   (124)

28   For an Altar Guild

Everlasting God, who callest us anew to worship and serve thee, we thank thee for the freedom and opportunity of worship. We praise thee for inspiring and challenging us in prayer and speech and song. Accept the devotion of our hearts and hands in this house as we prepare for the reverent worship of thy name.

Guide us in organizing and doing our work, recommending whatever improvements we may feel called upon to suggest, and relating ourselves to others in our church, that the beauty of holiness may truly be upon us as we bow before thy majesty; through Jesus Christ our Lord.   Amen.   (102)

Men's Groups

29   Show Us How to Work

Father of all men, through whose Son we all are brothers, praise be to thee for the wonders of the world about us and the mysteries of life within us. We thank thee for the privilege of service in thy church. Grant us insight to detect every opportunity to use our talents unselfishly, and show us how to work with one another in patience and mutual understanding for the advancement of thy kingdom; in the name of our elder brother, Jesus Christ our Lord. Amen.   (111)

30   Help Us to Follow

O God, our Lord and Creator, thou hast made man in thine own image, and though he has fallen into sin, thou hast said in thy Word, "It does not yet appear what we shall be." We thank thee that thou hast lifted us up out of the miry clay and set our feet on solid rock, and hast planted the marks of dignity and hope on human nature. Help us to give answer to thy redeeming love by yielding our lives to thee, devoting ourselves to the quest and doing of thy holy will, and following in the footsteps of the Lord Jesus, in whose name we pray.   Amen.   (138)

31   Make Us Dependable

God, our Lord, hear us thy people who come to thee again in the name of him who loved and loves us. Thou art our God and we are committed to thee, both in life and in death.

Thanks be unto thee for thy continued presence among us. We especially thank thee because thou hast given each of us important work to do for thee.

Grant that we may regard no job as mean, vulgar, or unimportant. Grant that we may deem no man unworthy of our love and respect. Keep us aware of the coming of thy kingdom.   Amen.   (60)

32   Help Us in Every Way

Lord of our lives, we bring our poor selves before thee again in common prayer. Though we are often poor and selfish, yet in the warmth and light of thy love we become true sons of thine, strong, purposeful, and of great tenderness in all of our dealings with each other.

As we worship thee and plan our work in thy church, give us the mind and heart of thy Son, Jesus Christ. In our discussions, may we be sincere and truth seeking; in our fellowship, gracious and forgiving; in our planning, wise and able; and in our daily walk, compassionate and honorable.

Send thy grace upon this working part of the great universal church. Show us, thy servants in thy church, our responsibility. Then teach us to rejoice in them and in thee.   Amen.   (60)

33   Give Us a Vision

Thou hast inspired men of old, O Lord, to labor in thy kingdom and work for the good of thy church in this world. Give us also, we pray thee, a vision of how we may fit our lives into thy plans for this world. Thou hast richly blessed our church, making it a place where hearts are united in devotion as they serve thee. Let our hearts find their deepest satisfaction in serving thee, as we do our part in thy great household of faith; through Jesus Christ our Lord.   Amen.   (104)

34   For the Wise Use of Knowledge

Almighty God, who hast given to men the capacity to search out and use the wonderful powers of thy universe, grant to us also the sense of responsibility and the wisdom to use those powers not for destruction but for the benefit of all mankind; for the sake of Jesus Christ our Lord.   Amen.   (27)

Families

35   Bless Every Home

Come, Lord Jesus, into every home. Be thou our guest, as long ago thou wast in Bethany. Make each family conscious of thy healing nearness. Open our eyes to thy eternal beauty, our ears to the whisper of thy will. Open our hearts to thy ceaseless love. Awaken in us such gratitude that every act is sacramental and every common task is done as unto thee. In thy dear name, we pray.   Amen.   (107)

36   For Parents

O God, who art the Father of all, we thank thee for permitting us to share in the joys and responsibilities of parenthood. Add to our natural love for our children, a zeal to inspire them with love of thee and devotion to thy cause in the world. May thy presence in our hearts so shine forth in our lives that our children will want to know and to serve thee all their lives. Through Jesus Christ our Lord, we pray.   Amen.   (97)

37   For the Aged

We pray thy blessing, O God, upon the aged; that the evening time of their lives, like the autumn leaves, may become more and more beautiful. May their homeward walk be joyous as they descend life's sunset slopes. Fill their souls with the radiant assurance of their eternal home.

We pray thy blessing also upon those who are caring for the aged and giving to them some of the tenderness which they crave at life's eventide. Encourage them to find pleasure in being able to serve thee in serving others.   Amen.   (149)

A Church Organization

38   Help Us to Follow

O Lord who art the head of thy church, send out upon us thy holy light as thou didst give light to thy first disciples, so that we may go as they did into all the ways of human activity to witness to thy truth and power. Give us the will to follow thee and the joy which comes of serving thee. Make our congregation and our fellowship a means of bringing thy kingdom into our community and our generation. Thine is the kingdom, the power, and the glory forever.   Amen. (9)

39   For All Groups

O God, who art ever working in men's hearts by the operation of thy Holy Spirit, to make us fellow workers with thy will, save us and keep us, we beseech thee,

   from all unwillingness to learn thy will,
   from clinging too much to our own plans and desires,
   from being afraid to follow thy leading.

from allowing our own ambitions to cloud the vision of thy will
   for us,
from fearing new truth and new ways of thought and life,
and from seeking to forward human progress by carrying out our
   own wills without seeking to know thine.
And then, as with the saints of old, comprehend all our needs with
thy amazing love and strengthening grace; through Jesus Christ, thy
Son, our Lord.   Amen.   (44)

40   For More Love and Faithfulness
Forgive us, good Lord, when we stumble along the way because we
have tried to follow thee only halfheartedly. Cleanse our hearts that
we may love thee more fully and serve thee more faithfully.   Amen.
                                                            (105)

41   Draw Us Closer to Thee
Our Father and our God, we thank thee for thy life with its beauty
and eternal power, which is all around us; for thy boundless love
which sent Jesus, our Savior, into the world; for his loving presence
in our hearts as we receive him.

   Let our minds rest in thee above all other thoughts, our Father,
as we meet and work together in this organization. Remind us that
fellowship in thy church is not only that of man to fellow man, but
that it is a high and holy fellowship through thee to others. Teach us
therefore, to lift every situation and each relationship into the light
of thy love. Keep us from relying upon our own wisdom and making
decisions without thee. Instead do thou move us in all we do to seek
thee first, to listen to thy will, and to follow thy leading.

   Fill us with thy Holy Spirit, forgive us, and use us! We humbly
pray in Jesus' name.   Amen.   (107)

42   For Unity in Diversity
We seek thy wisdom, O God, where our dreams for Christian service
are not alike. Be with every member of this meeting as we rejoice in

the health of differing opinions and the vigor of unbroken Christian love. We lay before thee the matters on our hearts. Teach us to seek thy will in patience and sustain us all in mutual service. We pray in the name of the Master who washed his disciples' feet and said, "Abide in my love."   Amen.   (55)

43   For Determination to Glorify God
O God, in whose service we find the most worthy pursuits of our lives, grant unto us, we beseech thee, the grace to persist in those activities which are to thy greater glory, leaving behind all such concerns as shall detract from the purpose for which we have been called out, even the bringing in of thy kingdom on earth as it is in heaven; to whom be all honor and glory in the church, world without end. Amen.   (95)

44   Help Us to Undergird the Work of the Church
O Thou, whose only begotten Son established for us the church through the lives of holy apostles, teach us that all we do in Christ's name must be rooted and grounded in that church. May we temper all of our thinking with a true knowledge of thy word. In our worship, may we be unconditionally faithful. As we give of our time, our talents, and our substance, may it be with singleness of heart. And so fulfill in us, as members of this [name of organization], that purpose which stands above all others in our undertaking, to undergird and strengthen the work of the church of Jesus Christ, in whose name we pray.   Amen.   (95)

Committee Meetings

45   For Harmony in Working Together
O God who art the Father of our Lord Jesus, it is good for us to be here with one another and with thee. Guide our thinking, bless our

plans, sanctify our fellowship. Give us a sense of community that we may cherish each other and work together in harmony for the extension of thy kingdom on earth. We pray thee to bless our church and pastor that they may be effective in saving souls and bringing light to dark places. Now to thee, we ascribe honor, praise, and glory. Amen.   (18)

46   For Alertness of Mind
Eternal God, whose purposes are ever larger than our minds can fathom, whose will for us is ever greater than our plans can encompass, yet whose grace lends mercy to our insufficiencies and shortcomings, we give thee praise for the vision and the trust that thou hast given to us. For the high calling of our discipleship, for the inspiration of prophets and martyrs who have gone before us, for the faithful witness of thy church to thy revelation in Jesus Christ, and for the urgent summons of our times, we thank thee. Grant us now, by thy Holy Spirit, consciences that are sensitive, minds that are alert, wills that are true, and hearts that are untiring and unafraid; through Jesus Christ our Lord.   Amen.   (56)

47   Help Us to Plan Humbly
Behold us, our Father, meeting in thy name as members of thy church, gathered from many households yet belonging to one body, acknowledging our separate responsibilities and limited perspectives yet owning one duty, divided in our interests yet claiming one supreme allegiance, as we seek to understand ourselves and our opportunities more clearly. May we bring the fullness of our wisdom to the task of seeking thine. May we plan humbly, yet knowing that men seek light from those who are illumined by Christ. So may we, not thinking too highly of ourselves, bear witness to thee and thy living power; through Jesus Christ our Lord.   Amen.   (56)

48   Renew Our Minds
Accept, O God, our thanks for the fellowship which is ours in thy church. As members of the Body of Christ, grant us more of his vision.

Cleanse our hearts of pride and selfishness. Renew our minds that we may think thy thoughts after thee. So capture our wills that we may become more worthy servants and more persuasive witnesses of thy grace; through Jesus Christ our Lord.   Amen.   (20)

49   Consecrate Us Anew

Creator of life, consecrate us anew in thy service. Use us to complete and perfect thy works in this world. Take our limited abilities and so multiply them by thy grace that we may be adequate to do thy will, not for any self glory, but to thy honor; through Christ our Lord.   Amen.   (123)

50   For the Sunshine of God's Love

Our Father who sendest the brightness of the sun to warm and heal and beautify the earth, send now the sunshine of thy love into our souls. Cleanse our hearts from every evil and selfish desire. Make this hour of fellowship with Christian friends a time of worshiping thee. In Jesus' name, we pray.   Amen.   (26)

51   For Eagerness to Help

Eternal Father, we are glad to be called into service in thy kingdom. Give us the vision to see what needs to be done, the eagerness to do whatever we can, and the joy that comes from seeing a task completed. May our efforts, aided by thy guidance, serve thy holy purposes and honor thy Son, in whose name we pray.   Amen.   (20)

52   For People Making Visits on Behalf of the Church

O Lord Jesus Christ, who didst come to seek and to save that which is lost, grant us more of thy concern for those who know thee not. Speak through us the inviting word; endow us with assurance to point those we visit to the incarnate word; and may the literate word of thy truth be on our lips. This we pray in thy holy name.   Amen.   (44)

53   We Yield Ourselves
Gracious Father, for this privilege of doing some small part of thy work in a corner of thy kingdom, we give thee thanks. We offer to thee the labor of our hands, the enthusiasm of our spirits, and the devotion of our hearts. Use us for thy cause as may seem fit and helpful in thy sight.   Amen.   (123)

Church School Teachers

54   For Teachers
Eternal God, who art the hope of the ends of the earth, and unto whom all flesh must come for salvation, we thank thee that thou hast called us into fellowship with thyself and hast given us a vision of service. As teachers of thy holy gospel, we would be taught of thee; as servants of thine, we would be rededicated to thee; as teachers of others, we would look upon our students with a desire to point them to the unsearchable riches of Christ. Through thy Holy Spirit empower us to discharge our tasks with diligence and with joy.   Amen.
(46)

55   For Teachers and Officers in Conference
O God our Father, the fountain of all light and truth, we are humbled by our calling to be leaders of the children, youth, and adults of the church. Fill us, we pray, with the spirit of the Master Teacher, that we may learn of him how to win our pupils to his high way of love and service. Help us to open the doors of abundant life for all those who are committed to our care; for the sake of thy kingdom of love.   Amen.   (111)

56   For Students and Teachers
O Thou who art the light of the minds that know thee, the life of the souls that love thee, and the strength of the thoughts that seek thee, be thou a living presence in hearts that need thee.

Grant all teachers and students to know that which is worth knowing, to love that which is worth loving, to praise that which pleaseth
thee most, and to dislike whatsoever is evil in thine eyes.

Grant them—and us—true judgment to distinguish things that
differ, and above all to search out and do what thou wouldst have
done; through Jesus Christ our Lord.   Amen.   (44)

57   For the Spirit of the Master

Give us thy spirit, O Christ, to make us teachers worthy of thy name.
Open our hearts and minds to a wider vision of our task. Arouse
within us the love and understanding required of Christian teachers.
And we ask that thou be with us as we strive to lead others to thy way
of life.   Amen.   (140)

58   For Humility and Understanding

Our Father, grant us the gift of laughter with children; the joy of
planning and working with them; the understanding that is needed
to accept each child into our love; the humility to learn from others
and from children.   Amen.   (78)

59   A Psalm of Vocation *(to be read responsively)*

My son, gather instruction from thy youth up:
And even unto gray hairs thou shalt find wisdom.
The life of him that laboreth, and is wise,
Shall be made sweet.
If a man love righteousness
The fruits of wisdom's labor are virtues,
For she teacheth soberness and understanding, righteousness and
    courage;
And there is nothing in life more profitable than these.
How shall he become wise that holdeth the plow,
That driveth oxen and is occupied with their labors?
He glorieth in the shaft of the goad;
He will set his heart upon turning his furrows.

So is the smith sitting by the anvil,
And considering the unwrought iron:
He will set his heart upon perfecting his works,
And he will be wakeful to adorn them perfectly.
So is the potter sitting at his work,
And turning the wheel about:
He will fashion the clay with his arm,
He will apply his heart to finish the glazing.
So is the teacher, instructing the young,
Loving wisdom, imparting the spirit of truth:
That our sons may be as plants
Grown up in their youth;
That our daughters may be as cornerstones,
Polished after the similitude of a palace.
They shall not labor in vain,
For their labor is with wisdom and with knowledge and with
* skillfulness.*
Without these shall not a city be inhabited,
And men shall not sojourn nor walk up and down therein.
For these maintain the fabric of the world;
And in the handiwork of their craft is their prayer. (137)

60   For Opening a Church School Class

O God of truth, in whom there is no darkness and who desirest that
all men shall come to the light, we thank thee for thy word which
makes plain our pathway; especially do we thank thee for him in
whom we see the true life to which thou hast called us and in and
through whom we see thyself in human form. Grant us to hear and to
see anew the truth that sets us free, and create within us that courage
to do the truth as we are given to see it; through Jesus Christ our
Lord.   Amen.   (46)

❋

Church Officers and Leaders

61   For Grace to Carry Out Duties

Eternal Father, who by thy spirit at work in the hearts of the early church didst set aside "seven men of good repute, full of the Spirit and of wisdom" to minister in routine duties, in order that our Lord's disciples might be unencumbered in their preaching ministry, we pray thy blessings upon the officers of this church. Give to them the spirit of Stephen and his six colleagues, who so faithfully accepted their vocation. Give each one to see that his task, even though at times seemingly small and undramatic, is a part of thy great kingdom's work. So with courage, patience, and devotion may all of our church leaders each day carry out their important duties. We pray in the name of him who has called us into a divine labor, Jesus Christ our Lord.   Amen.   (33)

62   Enlighten Us

O God of wisdom and light, upon whom we depend utterly, we praise and glorify thee. We thank thee for thy mysterious work in our lives, for using us—imperfect tools that we are—for tasks of thy kingdom.

Our Father, cleanse and enlighten us. Make us channels of thy love and thy will. Grant us the insight of Jesus to see hidden beauty in every life. Give us the gentle patience of Jesus to deal tenderly with others. Teach us to trust not in our efforts alone, but rather in thy eternal concern for all men.

Forgive us for every thought or deed which separates us from thee. Free us from an overweening desire for human praise, and call us to a greater service of thee. In Jesus' name, we pray.   Amen.   (107)

63   For a Group of Leaders

O Christ, our Lord and Head of the church, to thee be honor and glory in the church. Keep us, we beseech thee, from the prideful accent upon self which would overshadow thy saving grace in our hearts. Grant us strength that we may courageously and fearlessly serve thee within thy church. Fortify us in the faith made flesh in thee that we may mightily exalt thy name as living members of thy body and bear eloquent testimony to thy saving power which is thy free gift to all mankind.   Amen.   (73)

✳ 1184086

The Building of a Church

64   For the Consecration of a Building Committee

We thank thee, our heavenly Father, for the confidence placed in us, thy stewards, who will lead this congregation in the planning and construction of a new house of worship. Give us the wisdom and patience so necessary for the task. Supplement our desires with knowledge and understanding. And in all things make us conscious that except thou dost build the house, we labor in vain.   Amen.   (64)

65   For a Building Committee

Our dear heavenly Father, as thou hast built into the very structure of the universe thy redemptive purpose, so, as we plan an edifice to thy name's honor and glory, we would pray that it will never be a structure merely of wood, steel, and stone but a sanctuary where hungry souls will find peace, and where yearning souls may encounter thee and thy Son, Jesus Christ, our Lord, in whose name we pray. Amen.   (87)

66   A Daily Prayer for Church Members

We thank thee, Father, that thy perfect will is guiding us in planning, building, and paying for our new church. Express thyself through us that we may complete our task to thy glory and to the satisfaction of all concerned.   Amen.   (123)

✳

An Interchurch Group

67   For Willing Hearts

"I therefore, a prisoner for the Lord, beg you to lead a life worthy of the calling to which you have been called, with all lowliness and meekness, with patience, forbearing one another in love, eager to maintain the unity of the Spirit in the bond of peace."

Our Father in heaven, we thy children come before thee in the spirit of gratitude and praise. We thank thee that we may unite in a common cause. We rejoice that we may pray together and say, "Our Father." We thank thee that thy love is more inclusive, more universal, more forgiving and forbearing than our love. We must confess with shame that so often we are selfish and selective in whom we want to love, forgetting that we should love even as thou lovest. Impress indelibly upon our minds the challenge of our Master: "By this all men will know that you are my disciples, if you have love for one another."

Give us grace to see and wisdom to understand thy gracious will for the building of thy kingdom. Give us unity of purpose, open minds, and willing hearts to work together in the projects that can unite us and make our work for the kingdom more effective. Give us a wider vision to be able to see beyond the barriers of our own organizations which we have erected, and to be able to see the larger fields which are ripe for the harvest. Grant us grace and strength to lead a life worthy of the calling to which we have been called with all lowliness and meekness, eager to maintain the unity of the Spirit in the bond of peace.

We pray thee, O God, to bless us in Jesus' name and for his sake. Praise, glory, and honor be to the Father, the Son, and the Holy Spirit.   Amen.   (113)

❀

Community Gatherings

68   For Every Community

O God of our fathers, who from generation to generation hast watched over us in love, hear us in hours of perplexity and decision. Revive in us a spirit of devotion to the public good, that strife and tumult may cease, and justice and truth be exalted. Enable the people of this community and every community to live in good will and neighborliness, so that trusting in thee, we may grow in mutual understanding and love for each other; through Jesus Christ our Lord.   Amen.   (133 ad)

69   For a Church in Its Community Witness

O Thou who hast established thy church and purchased it with a price, not of silver nor of gold but with the precious blood of Christ, grant that our own church in this community may be the salt of the earth and as a city set on a hill whose light cannot be hid. Lead us in the doing of deeds of love and mercy. Move us to join with others in righting the wrongs and strengthening the rights that mark our common life. Grant that as thy word is preached, and as our people's work and witness are carried forward within these walls and in our daily walk, we may help to make our community a better, holier place for thy children to dwell in, and by so doing speed the day when thy kingdom shall come and thy will be done o'er all the earth; through Jesus Christ our Lord.   Amen.   (138)

70   A Prayer for Civic Assemblies

Eternal God, our Father, Source of wisdom and truth, we invoke thy blessing upon this assembly. Thou hast committed to us the solemn trust of life. Help us so to invest our time and talents that we may serve the common good. Make our lives meaningful so that they may be fulfilled in service. Above the smoke and dust of the city, help us to see the stars of our higher purposes. Help us to look beyond the advantage of the moment to see the welfare of our larger cause.

Dedicate us to the service of the common good. So may thy blessing rest upon our community, to make it great. In the Master's name, we pray.   Amen.   (119)

The Close of a Meeting

71   For Full Success
Our heavenly Father, thou hast been with us during this time of deliberation and planning in behalf of thy church and its work; and now, as we go forth to serve, be thou with us, that all of our most earnest endeavors for thee may meet with full success, and through us, others may be blessed. In Christ's name, we pray.   Amen.   (90)

72   Enable Us to Help Others
Omnipotent God, thou who hast created us and sustained us to this hour, come into our hearts just now with thy power and divine energy that we may go out into this troubled and sorrow-filled world to comfort, to bless, to lift burdens, and to bring hope to those who linger near despair. May we always be about our Father's business, realizing that Christ has no hands but our hands to do his work today. In his name, we pray.   Amen.   (90)

4

A Treasury of Devotional Aids

※

Opening Sentences or Calls to Worship

73   Psalm 95:6-7
O come, let us worship and bow down,
Let us kneel before the Lord, our Maker!
For he is our God, and we are the people of his pasture, and the
sheep of his hand.

74   Psalm 145:17-19
The Lord is just in all his ways, and kind in all his doings.
The Lord is near to all who call upon him, to all who call upon
him in truth.
(Unison) He fulfills the desire of all who fear him, he also hears
their cry, and saves them.

75   Isaiah 55:6-7
Seek the Lord while he may be found,
Call upon him while he is near;
Let the wicked forsake his way,
And the unrighteous man his thoughts;
Let him return to the Lord, that he may have mercy on him,
And to our God, for he will abundantly pardon.

76   Psalm 51:1-4a

Have mercy upon me, O God, according to thy steadfast love;
According to thy abundant mercy blot out my transgressions.

Wash me thoroughly from my iniquity, and cleanse me from my sin!

For I know my transgressions, and my sin is ever before me.

Against thee, thee only, have I sinned, and done that which is evil in thy sight.

77   1 John 1:8-9

If we say we have no sin, we deceive ourselves, and the truth is not in us.

If we confess our sins, he is faithful and just, and will forgive our sins and cleanse us from all unrighteousness.

78   Habakkuk 2:20

The Lord is in his holy temple; let all the earth keep silence before him.

(A moment of silence follows.)

In the name of the Father, and of the Son, and of the Holy Spirit. Amen.

Opening Prayers or Invocations

79   Help Us to Seek

O Lord our God, who art always more ready to bestow thy good gifts upon us than we are to seek them, help us so to seek that we may truly find, so to ask that we may joyfully receive, so to knock that the door of thy mercy may be opened to us. Through Jesus Christ our Lord, we pray.   Amen.   (13)

80   General Confession

O almighty God, Giver of all grace, who pourest out on all who desire it the spirit of grace and supplication, deliver us, when we draw nigh to thee, from coldness of heart and wanderings of mind, that with steadfast thoughts and kindled affections we may worship thee in spirit and in truth. Through Jesus Christ our Lord, we pray. Amen.   (17 ad)

81   Cleanse Our Minds and Hearts

O Lord, our God, who art the life of all, the help of those who flee unto thee, and the hope of those who cry unto thee, look mercifully upon us! Cleanse our minds and hearts that with a clear conscience and a calm hope we may confidently worship thee; through Jesus Christ our Lord.   Amen.   (25)

82   Inspire Us

Almighty God, unto whom all hearts are open, all desires known, and from whom no secrets are hid, cleanse the thoughts of our hearts by the inspiration of thy Holy Spirit, that we may perfectly love thee, and worthily magnify thy holy name. Through Jesus Christ our Lord, we pray.   Amen.   (38)

83   For Greater Devotion

O God, who art the source of all wisdom, the fountain of all good, and the goal of all our striving, we acknowledge thee to be the inspiration and consummation of our gathering here; be pleased to accept our gratitude and to grant us a fuller knowledge of thee, a greater devotion to thee, and a deeper love for the work of thy kingdom. Through Jesus Christ our Lord, we pray.   Amen.   (46)

84   For Divine Blessing

Our Father, from whom we have the gift of this new day, grant us thy blessing as we seek thy presence in worship. Lead us to thyself by the quiet way of prayer, by the high road of faith, and by the inward path of love. In Jesus' name, we pray.   Amen.   (59)

85   Opportunities for Service

Dear Lord, as we begin our meeting we turn again to thee in faith and hope and love. Make us thankful for all thy mercies and especially today for the opportunities for service that are ours. Make us strong not only to carry the burden of our own tasks, but help us to reach out our hands in love to folks who need our help and whom we can help. Teach us not to be sad when our own plans fail to reach the goals we dream of, nor yet too glad when thou dost let a good hope come true for us. Forgive us our sins and use us fruitfully in thy good cause; for Jesus' sake.   Amen.   (34)

86   Direct Our Thoughts

Eternal God, Lord of all life, we bow before thee in adoration and lift up our hearts to thee in praise. Lead us in our deliberations; counsel us with thy wisdom. Make us keenly aware of our helplessness without thee. Direct our thoughts, our words, our deeds that thy will may be done and not our own. So may thy glory be revealed in the love and obedience of thy servants. Through Jesus Christ our Lord, we pray.   Amen.   (73)

87   For Thy Larger Family *(to be read responsively)*

O God, who hast been the fortress and defense of all who have put their trust in thee throughout all ages and in all places, we thank thee that we are members of thy great family.

We thank thee, O God, that thou art our loving and merciful Father!

We praise thee that we may feel united in spirit with all who love thee and who seek to worship thee in spirit and truth.

We praise thee for the fellowship of all who love thee, our Father!

Forgive us our many sins that tend to separate us from thee and from one another; help us to remember that only as we love each other do we truly love thee; bless every movement and every effort to unite thy children; enable us to grow in grace and in the knowledge of our one Lord and Savior.

Pardon our many sins, our merciful Father; establish and confirm us in all that pleases thee. Unite all thy people in a growing fellowship of grace. Through Jesus Christ our Lord, we pray. Amen. (145)

88 An Invocation and Confession for Evening

O Thou whose chosen dwelling is the heart that longs for thy presence and humbly seeks thy face; we come to thee as the day declines and the shadows of evening fall. Deepen within us the sense of shame and sorrow for the wrongs we have done, for the good we have left undone; and strengthen every desire to amend our lives according to thy holy will. Restore to us the joy of thy salvation; bind up that which is broken; give light to our minds, strength to our wills, and rest to our souls; according to thy loving-kindness in Jesus Christ our Lord. Amen. (1)

❉

Prayers of Humility and Confession

89 Forgive What We Have Been

Our heavenly Father, who by thy love hast made us, and through thy love hast kept us, and in thy love wouldst make us perfect, we humbly confess that we have not loved thee with all our heart and soul and mind and strength, and that we have not loved one another as Christ hath loved us. Forgive us for what we have been; help us to amend what we are; and with thy Holy Spirit direct what we shall become; through Jesus Christ our Lord. Amen. (14)

90 Perfect Us

O thou Spirit of holiness and truth, who dost ever move to fashion all things complete and whole, in thy presence we see the imperfections around us; by thy light we are ashamed of the darkness of our own hearts. We have fallen short of the fullness of life that might be in us. We have not enough served the unfinished works of light in the world of men and nations. Help us here to see the brightness of thy glory, that all our days we may steadfastly seek the health and wholeness of our fellow men.   Amen.   (137)

91   Confession of Sin

Lord of all might and compassion, who knowest our frame and re-memberest our weaknesses, we humbly confess the evil we have done and our weariness in well-doing, the vows we have broken, the duties we have refused, the hours we have lightly spent without any gracious deed, the tasks undone which proclaim us idle and unprofitable serv-ants, and all our many transgressions, shortcomings, and offenses. Have compassion on our unworthiness, we beseech thee; create in us a sincere desire for whatsoever things are true, just, honorable, pure, and of good report; mold us inwardly to thy will; so unite us with thyself in love and confidence that whatever thou withholdest we may cheerfully resign, whatever thou commandest we may dili-gently perform, and whatever thou bestowest we may gratefully use; and in the end be more than conquerors through him who loved us and gave himself for us.   Amen.   (22)

92   Deliver Us

From the blindness that will not know thee, from the pride that will not serve thee, and from the perverseness that will not love thee, de-liver us, we beseech thee, O almighty and ever-gracious Father, and so draw us to thyself that through all the coming days we may live in obedience to thy holy laws, in charity and long-suffering, and in the full assurance of thy heavenly kingdom. Through Jesus Christ our Lord, we pray.   Amen.   (22)

93   Penitence and Confession

O thou to whom men in every generation have come, we humble our hearts in sincere penitence and confession before thee. We bring to thee these lives of ours: their selfishness, their love of the unlovely, and their hunger for the good, the true, and the pure. We plead thy forgiveness for the day's wrongs and crave thy pardon and peace.

Hear our unexpressed prayers, those deep aspirations of our souls that we cannot put into words, and grant, we beseech thee, the consciousness of thy constant presence. Through Jesus Christ our Lord, we pray. Amen. (77)

94 For Forgiveness and Strength (*to be read responsively*)
Let us draw near to the throne of God with reverent and believing hearts.

Thou great and glorious King, Ruler of heaven and earth, who art clothed with honor and majesty, look with thy favor upon us as we approach thy throne of grace, and grant us a lively sense of thy presence.

In thy mercy hear us, O Lord!

Thou, O most merciful God, art gracious, slow to anger, and of great loving-kindness. Thou dealest with us as with children, and receivest us whenever we come to thee with contrite hearts.

O Lord, thou art good to all!

Thou hast shown thy boundless love in the giving of thine only Son. For his sake we beseech thee to pardon our many transgressions of thy holy will and to forgive us our shortcomings. Free us from the power of sin, that we may serve thee in purity of heart.

Hear our confession, our gracious Father, and in mercy pardon us and restore us as thy children!

We praise thee, O Father, for thine infinite love, which offers us and all mankind salvation in Christ. We bless thee for giving us thy Holy Spirit, who seeks us when we go astray. Bring us ever more completely under his control, that his power may work through us to overcome our weaknesses, to the glory of thy holy name.

In thee do we trust, our Father! Accept us, help us, strengthen us, defend us! Hear thou our prayers and receive our praise. Through Jesus Christ our Lord, we pray. Amen. (145)

❋

Affirmations of Faith

AFFIRMATIONS such as the Apostles' Creed may be found in the worship section of most hymnals. Here are five others that may be used:

95   Statement of Faith

We believe in God, the Eternal Spirit, Father of our Lord Jesus
Christ and our Father, and to his deeds we testify:
He calls the worlds into being,
　　creates man in his own image
　　and sets before him the ways of life and death.
He seeks in holy love to save all people from aimlessness and sin.
He judges men and nations by his righteous will
　　declared through prophets and apostles.
In Jesus Christ, the man of Nazareth, our crucified and risen Lord,
　　he has come to us
　　and shared our common lot,
　　conquering sin and death
　　and reconciling the world to himself.
He bestows upon us his Holy Spirit,
　　creating and renewing the church of Jesus Christ,
　　binding in covenant faithful people of all ages, tongues, and
　　　races.
He calls us into his church
　　to accept the cost and joy of discipleship,
　　to be his servants in the service of men,
　　to proclaim the gospel to all the world
　　and resist the powers of evil,
　　to share in Christ's baptism and eat at his table,
　　to join him in his passion and victory.
He promises to all who trust him
　　forgiveness of sins and fullness of grace,
　　courage in the struggle for justice and peace,
　　his presence in trial and rejoicing,

and eternal life in his kingdom which has no end.

Blessing and honor, glory and power be unto him.   Amen.   (57)

96   Affirmation for Our Church

Let us have a church that dares imitate the heroism of Jesus; that seeks inspiration as he sought it; that judges the past as he; that acts on the present as Jesus did; that prays as he prayed; that works as he worked; that lives as he lived. Let us have a church for the whole man: truth for the mind, good works for the hands, love for the heart; and for the soul, that aspiration after perfection, that unfaltering faith in God, which, like lightning in the clouds, shines brightest when elsewhere it is darkest.   (96)

97   United in Faith

We are united in the efforts of faith: faith in *truth*, in the growth of knowledge and of understanding; faith in *love*, in the labors and rewards of friendly living; faith in *people*, in the powers of men to build an earthly commonwealth of freedom and of peace; faith in *life*, the life of all things that is the life of God, whose service is perfect freedom, whose presence is fullness of joy.   (137)

98   We Believe

We believe in God the Father, God the Son, and God the Holy Spirit —our Maker, Redeemer, and Enlightener—who is almighty, eternal, and merciful.

We believe in prayer and the sacraments, in divine support and Christlike living, in doing our part sincerely and faithfully, trusting in God's grace in this world and hoping for it in the world to come.   Amen.   (102)

99   The Person of Jesus Christ

I believe that Jesus Christ is true God and true man in one Person —my Savior, Redeemer, and Lord.   Amen.   (31)

✺

Scripture with Hymn Responses

100   God's Holiness and Majesty

In the year that King Uzziah died I saw the Lord sitting upon a throne, high and lifted up; and his train filled the temple. Above him stood the seraphim; each had six wings: with two he covered his face, and with two he covered his feet, and with two he flew. And one called to another and said:

"Holy, holy, holy is the Lord of hosts; the whole earth is full of his glory."

And the foundations of the thresholds shook at the voice of him who called, and the house was filled with smoke. And I said: "Woe is me! For I am lost; for I am a man of unclean lips, and I dwell in the midst of a people of unclean lips; for my eyes have seen the King, the Lord of hosts!"

Holy, holy, holy! Lord God of hosts!
Heaven and earth are full of thee!
Heaven and earth are praising thee,
O Lord most high!
(Refrain of "Day Is Dying in the West")

Then flew one of the seraphim to me, having in his hand a burning coal which he had taken with tongs from the altar. And he touched my mouth, and said: "Behold, this has touched your lips; your guilt is taken away, and your sin forgiven." And I heard the voice of the Lord saying, "Whom shall I send, and who will go for us?" Then I said, "Here I am! Send me."

O Master, let me walk with thee
In lowly paths of service free;
Tell me thy secret, help me bear
The strain of toil, the fret of care.

101   Jesus Christ as Ruler

Give the king thy justice, O God, and thy righteousness to the royal son! May he judge thy people with righteousness, and thy poor with justice! Let the mountains bear prosperity for the people, and the hills, in righteousness!

May he live while the sun endures, and as long as the moon, throughout all generations! May he be like rain that falls on the mown grass, like showers that water the earth! In his days may righteousness flourish, and peace abound, till the moon be no more!

May he have dominion from sea to sea, and from the River to the ends of the earth!

> *Jesus shall reign where'er the sun*
> *Does his successive journeys run;*
> *His kingdom stretch from shore to shore,*
> *Till moons shall wax and wane no more.*

Blessed be the Lord, the God of Israel, who alone does wondrous things. Blessed be his glorious name for ever; may his glory fill the whole earth! Amen and Amen!

> *For him shall endless prayer be made,*
> *And praises throng to crown his head,*
> *His name, like sweet perfume, shall rise*
> *With every morning sacrifice.*

May the kings of Tarshish and of the isles render him tribute, may the kings of Sheba and Seba bring gifts! May all kings fall down before him, all nations serve him!

> *People and realms of every tongue*
> *Dwell on his love with sweetest song,*
> *And infant voices shall proclaim*
> *Their early blessings on his name.*

May he defend the cause of the poor of the people, give deliverance to the needy, and crush the oppressor!

For he delivers the needy when he calls, the poor and him who has no helper. He has pity on the weak and the needy, and saves the lives of the needy. From oppression and violence he redeems their life; and precious is their blood in his sight.

Blessings abound where'er he reigns;
The prisoner leaps to lose his chains;
The weary find eternal rest,
And all the sons of want are blest.

Long may he live, may gold of Sheba be given to him! May prayer be made for him continually, and blessings invoked for him all the day! May there be abundance of grain in the land; on the tops of the mountains may it wave; may its fruit be like Lebanon; and may men blossom forth from the cities like the grass of the field! May his name endure for ever, his fame continue as long as the sun! May men bless themselves by him, all nations call him blessed!

Let every creature rise and bring
Peculiar honors to our King;
Angels descend with songs again,
And earth repeat the loud Amen!   (110)

102   The Church

We, though many, are one body in Christ, and individually members one of another.

For no other foundation can anyone lay than that which is laid, which is Jesus Christ.

The church's one foundation
Is Jesus Christ her Lord;
She is his new creation
By water and the word:
From heaven he came and sought her
To be his holy bride;
With his own blood he bought her,
And for her life he died.

After this I looked, and behold, a great multitude which no man could number, from every nation, from all tribes and peoples and tongues, standing before the throne and before the Lamb, clothed in white robes, with palm branches in their hands.

Elect from every nation,
Yet one o'er all the earth,
Her charter of salvation
One Lord, one faith, one birth;
One holy name she blesses,
Partakes one holy food,
And to one hope she presses,
With every grace endued.

Christ loved the church and gave himself up for her, that he might sanctify her, having cleansed her by the washing of water with the word, that the church might be presented before him in splendor, without spot or wrinkle or any such thing, that she might be holy and without blemish.

'Mid toil and tribulation,
And tumult of her war,
She waits the consummation
Of peace forevermore;
Till with the vision glorious
Her longing eyes are blest,
And the great church victorious
Shall be the church at rest.

Then one of the elders addressed me saying, "Who are these, clothed in white robes, and whence have they come?" . . . "These are they who have come out of the great tribulation; they have washed their robes and made them white in the blood of the Lamb."

Yet she on earth hath union
With God the Three in One,
And mystic sweet communion
With those whose rest is won:
O happy ones and holy!
Lord, give us grace that we,
Like them, the meek and lowly,
On high may dwell with thee.

103   God in Nature

O Lord, our Lord, how majestic is thy name in all the earth!

For the beauty of the earth,
For the glory of the skies,
For the love which from our birth
Over and around us lies,
Lord of all, to thee we raise
This our hymn of grateful praise.

The heavens are telling the glory of God; and the firmament proclaims his handiwork.

Day to day pours forth speech, and night to night declares knowledge.

For the wonder of each hour,
Of the day and of the night,
Hill and vale, and tree and flower,
Sun and moon, and stars of light,
Lord of all, to thee we raise
This our hymn of grateful praise.

I will give thanks to the Lord with my whole heart;
I will tell of all thy wonderful deeds.
I will be glad and exult in thee, I will sing praise to thy name, O Most High.

For the joy of ear and eye;
For the heart and mind's delight;
For the mystic harmony
Linking sense to sound and sight:
Lord of all, to thee we raise
This our hymn of grateful praise. Amen.

✻

Prayers for the Church

104   A Prayer for Our Denomination

O God, our Father, who hast called the church to be thy living witness, we ask thy blessing to rest upon the work of our denomination. We thank thee for the fellowship in which we share and for the noble tradition which is ours. Make us ever ready to serve the larger interests of thy kingdom, and save us from the narrow view. May we be ready, if need be, to give up our own lives for the achievement of the larger unity of thy church. Keep us from pride and from narrowness, and make us ever ready to serve in the cause of Christ, at home and abroad.   Amen.   (119)

105   Speak Through Our Fellowship

Dear God, as we pray for our own individual needs, we lift our voices also in prayer for our denomination. Speak through our fellowship to the world's needs and bind us together to do thy will. Through Jesus Christ our Lord, we pray.   Amen.   (43)

106   For the Whole Church Throughout All the World

O thou who art the Shepherd of men's souls, and who watchest over thy flocks though they are scattered on a thousand hillsides, we rejoice in the teaching of thy Word that thou hast made of one blood all nations of men to dwell upon all the face of the earth, and that in Christ there can be neither Jew nor Greek, barbarian nor Scythian, bond nor free, since all are one in him. We penitently confess the unhappy divisions among thy people which have weakened their witness to the world and violated their kinship to one another as members of thy household of faith. We rejoice that in our time thou art drawing thy children together. Bless thou the World and the National Councils of Churches in so far as they honor thee and serve to strengthen thy cause in the world. Grant that we and all thy children may work together increasingly for thy kingdom and the gospel's sake, and thus discover anew that as we have one Lord, one

faith, one baptism, and one God and Father of all, so are we one
in Christ Jesus our Lord, in whose blessed name we pray.   Amen.
(138)

107   For Our Heritage of Faith

Dear Father, we lift our voices in thanksgiving for the heritage of
faith that we have received. May we, the children of our heroic
fathers, be no less devoted, courageous, and loyal than were they. Use
our denomination that thy will may be done and thy kingdom may
come. Through Jesus Christ our Lord, we pray.   Amen.

108   For Our Congregation and Denomination

O Father, we are humbled as we recall those through whose faithfulness we have received the gospel. They are always an unseen cloud
of witnesses about us. In our day we too would witness to this same
truth. Make us instruments in thy hands for the doing of thy will.
Use this congregation and our church that the Christ may be exalted
and his will accomplished. In his name, we pray.   Amen.   (43)

109   For Our Association or Fellowship

Gracious Father, may our association be touched with thy Holy
Spirit, to the end that we shall exemplify thy purpose.   Amen. (131)

110   For the Faithful Workers of Our Church

Lord of all power and grace, we thank thee for the devoted band of
men and women in this place who serve thee in season and out of
season. We remember all who labor with head and heart and hand
to build the church, to lead the young, to organize activities, and to
render a ministry of helpfulness. Enrich them abundantly with thy
Holy Spirit that in all their labors they may be strengthened and
Christ be glorified forever.   Amen.   (62)

111   For Church Unity

O God, give unto all who seek thy good pleasure such grace that the
bonds of peace in the unity of the Spirit may be kept. And grant

most speedily a vision to thy children of the good they may do if they unite in strength against the powers of evil. Inspire thy churches to unite in essential matters, according to thy fatherly desires. Help the church, like a mighty army, to move with power against all that is wrong and unfair; and empower us in every good thing to do thy will. These prayers we offer in the name of thy Son, that the day may soon come when there shall be one flock throughout the world, under one Shepherd. Amen. (103)

112 For Church Union

O thou living God, eternal Father, in whom our very being is grounded, in whom every living man in the world today has his existence, we pray to thee, thou hearer and answerer of prayer, thou awakener of desires that must rise to thee.

We thank thee for having brought us to this hour and day; for the blessings of rest of the night now past; for this new day with its many opportunities. We beseech thee to look down upon us this day. Pour thine own spirit upon our hearts, that spirit of sorrow and of love, of personal penitence and personal confidence, of personal humility and yet of personal and ambitious devotion.

Thou knowest the cause which has brought us together, members of two communions, feeling the compulsion of removing barriers which momentarily separate us, and thus keep us from fulfilling the Master's prayer, "That they may all be one." We need so much the guidance of thy Holy Spirit, in our planning, our understanding of one another, our reaching for the vision of great things to be accomplished, as we look forward to the consummation of our union.

O God, who didst so love the world, who hast not withheld the greatest of all conceivable deeds of love from man, do thou look down in thy mercy upon the nations of the world, upon all the distractions and class hatreds within Christendom. Let men not forget that the centuries have fled, and that Christ's name has been stamped upon their names. We confess with shame and sorrow the divisions and the hatreds which mar the name of Christendom. O Lord, forgive. Cleanse the heart of Christendom, that we may be ashamed that the dominion of Christ has not been fully accepted even among ourselves. Help us in our purposes and planning to take such steps as will remove the barriers of separation which have kept our respective church bodies apart.

Heavenly Father, beyond all our dreaming and asking, beyond all our vision and faith, do thou continue to act. Answer our prayers; fulfill our purposes; reveal thy glories; establish thy kingship over the hearts of men. All this we ask in the name of him who is our Lord, our Savior, even Jesus Christ, son of man and Son of God. Amen.   (40)

*

Evangelism

113   For the Church's Mission

Almighty God, whose compassions fail not, and whose loving-kindness reaches unto the world's end; we give thee humble thanks for all the great things thou hast done and art doing for the children of men; for the opening of distant lands to the light of thy truth; for making paths in the deep waters and highways in the desert; for knitting nation to nation in the bond of fellowship, and for the planting of thy church in all the earth. O merciful Father, in whom the whole family in heaven and earth is named, fill our hearts with grateful love for this thy goodness, granting us henceforth to serve thee better and more perfectly to know thee; through Jesus Christ our Lord.   Amen.   (1)

114   Help Us to Share

O thou God of the universe, who in thy great compassion hast given thy Son for man's redemption, we bless and thank thee for the experience of his saving power in our lives. Grant now, that we shall not selfishly retain this knowledge unto ourselves, but take advantage of every opportunity to speak a good word for our Lord and share the Christ, the best we have, with others. Help us to be zealous and winsome witnesses of his lifting, saving grace. In his name, we pray. Amen. (114)

115 Help Us to Serve

Unto thee, O gracious God, we come for divine infilling. Our lives are so devoid of spiritual power that our efforts in seeking to carry out thy purposes for us are often unavailing. Fit us by thy grace, both in spirit and ability to live helpfully with others. Give us an alertness to see and to accept the opportunities of service as they confront us, and may we do all in the name of Christ, whom we love and seek to serve. Amen. (114)

Stewardship

116 Teach Us to Serve

Teach us, good Lord, to serve thee as thou deservest; to give and not to count the cost; to fight and not to heed the wounds; to toil and not to seek for rest; to labor and not to ask for any reward, save that of knowing that we do thy will. Through Jesus Christ our Lord, we pray. Amen. (68)

117 Teach Us to Be Useful

Lord of all pots and pans and things, teach us that Christian work is as sacred as Christian worship; that the keys on a typewriter may be used to the glory of God as well as the keys on a pipe organ; that one purpose of organizations in thy church is to enable each of us to practice his worth in thy sight, O Lord, and show forth the sacredness of personality. Remind and show us all, O Holy Spirit of sanity, love, and peace, how to practice our profession of Christian love and forgiveness by working together for the common causes of thy kingdom. Teach us each one how to become a channel of thy grace. In the name of Christ, we pray. Amen. (10)

118   Help Us to Work

O Lord, in whom we live and move and have our being, keep us alert in mind, sweet in disposition, radiant in spirit, and agreeable to work wholeheartedly even with those whose ways are not always like ours and whose plans are different from any we would make. Help us to love thee so deeply that we shall love all thy people sincerely. For Christ's sake, we pray.   Amen.   (82)

119   Help Me to Serve Faithfully

Almighty God, Giver of all natural and spiritual life, fill my body with thy strength, direct my mind by thy Holy Spirit, and perfect my soul through Jesus Christ that I may at this time offer thee a true devotion and commitment of my Christian life, and persevere in my sincere resolution to serve thee more and more faithfully.   Amen.

(11)

120   For Complete Dedication

Almighty God, who hast thought nothing too good for us thy children, in that thou hast sent thy Son into the world to show us the completeness of thy love, we pray that we may evermore love thee and serve thy children, the people of thy world, in the complete dedication of all that we have and are.   Amen.   (47)

121   For Consecration

For eyes that see beauty in thy creation round about; for ears that hear the harmonies of heaven; for minds alert to thy truth; for consciences sensitive to thy direction; for hands that willingly serve thee in any way thou commandest, we pray thee, our Lord.   Amen.   (45)

122   Thanks for Opportunities of Service

We thank thee, Lord, for calling us into avenues of fellowship and service. Whatever the tasks before us, we would accept them as a challenge from thee. In every Christian labor, we are conscious of the great number of our fellow Christians who are colaborers together with us. Even more would we recognize the real presence of our Lord Jesus, who has said, "Lo, I am with you always."   Amen.

(45)

123   Living Sacrifices
Graciously give ear to our supplications. Breathe upon us the spirit of brotherhood; renew in us a clean heart and sound mind; draw us nearer to thee in the bonds of love and truth; and consecrate our desire to present ourselves as living sacrifices to thee. And we shall praise thee all the days of our life. Through Jesus Christ our Lord, we pray.   Amen.   (103 ad)

124   Inspire Us to Serve Cheerfully
O God, who dost require service while it is day, before the night comes when no man can work, help us to devote our lives in loyal service unto thee. Save us from sowing sparingly, that we may reap bountifully from thy mercy. Make us cheerful givers of our time, talents, and possessions. Through him who came to serve and to give his life for many, even Jesus Christ our Lord, we pray.   Amen. (102)

125   Prayer for the Every Member Canvass
Almighty God, our heavenly Father, make us conscious as we visit from home to home, seeking the consecration of lives and dollars for the work of thy church, that we go as ambassadors of thy kingdom. Instill in us the proper concept of Christian stewardship that the members we reach may be moved to open their hearts and their purposes to make possible the enlarging of the program of the church of Christ in our own community and throughout the world.   Amen.

(64)

❋

Personal Prayers

126   Prayer of Francis of Assisi

     Lord, make me an instrument of thy peace;
     Where there is hatred, let me sow love;
     Where there is injury, pardon;
     Where there is doubt, faith;
     Where there is despair, hope;
     Where there is darkness, light; and
     Where there is sadness, joy.

127   Remake Us

Almighty and everlasting Father, who didst send thy Son into the world for our redemption, so remake us that we may be empowered to do thy will, for thy glory and our eternal salvation. Through Jesus Christ our Lord, we pray.   Amen.   (102)

128   For Wisdom

     God, give us the serenity to accept what cannot be changed;
     Give us the courage to change what should be changed;
     Give us the wisdom to distinguish one from the other.   (85)

129   For a Charitable Mind

Deliver us, O Lord, from reckless judgments on each other's motives, from hasty and heartless generalizations, and from all sham. Increase in us the gifts and graces of patience, gentleness, and forgiveness, and help us to view all persons and issues in the light of our Savior's cross.   Amen.   (100)

130   For Trust in God's Care

We put our trust in thy goodness, O Lord. Our way is clear before thee. Thou knowest every violent storm, every chilling wind, every fearful darkness. We are but children and need the support of thine everlasting arms. Take our hand in thine. Lead us along the path with confidence. And bring us to our goal in joy. We ask it in the Savior's name.   Amen.   (37)

131   Help Us to Trust

Heavenly Father, thy love is light, thy will is peace, thy truth is liberty, thy service is joy. Make us eager to obey in order that we may truly be free. Grant that we may always be wise enough to trust the highest, knowing, however, that our clearest vision is but a dim image and an after-gleam of thy greatness and of thy truth. We ask it in the name of Jesus, our Lord and our Savior.   Amen.   (59)

132   For Those Who Are Disquieted

Regard, O Lord, with thy fatherly compassion all who are disquieted and tense, who cannot lose themselves either in happy work by day or in restful sleep by night, who looking within do not know themselves and looking to thee do not find thee. Lead them, we pray thee, out of clangor into quietude, out of futility into usefulness, out of despair into the sure serenity of truth. Teach them to believe that thou art faithful, and that thy charity hopeth all things and endureth all things; that all the darkness of the world, even the inner blackness of the soul, cannot quench one small candle of fidelity. Give them of thy perspective, thy humor, thy gift of tranquillity and poise. Be so firm that they may lean on thee; so persistent in leading that they may venture out and find pasture in the sunny fields of thy kingdom, where all who follow thy shepherding may find gladness and delight; in the name of earth's most calm and daring Son, Word of God and Master of men, our Savior Jesus Christ.   Amen.
                                                                 (120)

133   For Grace to Seek the Kingdom

Almighty God, Father of our spirits, in whom we live, move, and have our being, pour thy love into our hearts, we beseech thee, and cause thy heavenly grace to abound in us; that casting away all anxious thought for the things of this world we may seek first thy kingdom and righteousness, and labor to accomplish thy work. Through Jesus Christ our Lord, we pray.   Amen.   (128)

134   For Help in Time of Temptation

O God of power, who wilt not permit us to be tempted beyond our strength, guide us day by day that we may guard our thoughts and ask for strength in time of weakness. Above all, give us commanding convictions that we may not fall but endure faithfully to the end. Through Jesus Christ our Lord, we pray.   Amen.   (102)

135   Victory over Temptation

Almighty God, the source of all wisdom and the fountain of all truth, we come into thy presence in humble adoration. Grant us, we beseech thee, the insight that will enable us to recognize temptations in whatever disguises they may come to us, before we are ensnared by them. Give us the power that we may overcome all temptations which seek to entice us from the path of goodness and mercy, truth and justice. Help us so to live that we may do thy will here on earth, even as it is done in heaven. For Christ's sake, we pray.   Amen. (104)

136   Guidance

Give us grace, O Lord our God, to respond to the promptings of thy Holy Spirit within us. Direct us in the path which leads into the fullness of life.

We do not ask thee to make life easy; we pray only that thou wilt make it good. We do not seek to be relieved from our burdens and responsibilities; we ask thee for strength equal to the demands that are made upon us.

Renew our spirit, lest we become weary in well-doing, and refresh our heart that we may always be ready to do thy will. In Jesus' name, we pray.   Amen.   (104)

137   Courage

When the pressures of life weigh heavily upon us and our hearts sink within us, grant us, O Lord, thy grace that we may obtain new courage. It is thy presence which makes us strong and it is thy grace which sustains us. Encircled by a sense of thy love, may we become inspired to wrestle with our problems afresh with renewed hope. Let thy blessing rest upon the labors of our hands and the thoughts of our hearts. We pray in the name of Jesus.   Amen.   (104)

138   Friendship with God and Man

Eternal God, our Creator and our Lord, we thank thee for opening the door of the spirit through which we may come to thee at all times and enter into fellowship with thee. In thy presence there is fullness of joy. Thou hast made us for thyself; and as we enter into fellowship with thee, our restless hearts find rest and peace. Through thy grace may we extend our friendship to others, as we experience fellowship with thee. May no barrier separate us from any member of thy great household which includes all the children of men. In Jesus' name, we pray.   Amen.   (104)

139   For Additional Strength

When burdens bear down upon us testing our faith and stretching our patience, may we call to remembrance that our Lord never lays upon us crosses heavier than we are able to bear. We glory in the assurance that with every additional burden comes the blessing of additional strength. For the source of our hope and faith, even Jesus Christ, we give thanks to thee, O God.   Amen.   (45)

Prayers for Guidance

140   John Oxenham's Prayer

Our Father in heaven, we pray thee to send into our hearts, and into the hearts of all men everywhere, the spirit of our Lord Jesus Christ. Amen.

141   Grant Us a Pure Religion

Grant to us, dear Father in heaven, a pure religion. Give each of us the spirit of gentleness and love for our fellow men. Guard our hearts and minds that we may control our words and deeds. Ever give to us the desire to practice mercy among the needy. For Jesus' sake, we pray.   Amen.   (103)

142   Thanks for the Glory of Nature

O God of infinite power, help us to ascribe to thee all the glory and honor due to thy holy name. Cause us to remember thy goodness as we see glimpses of thy greatness in the growth of grass, the beauty of flowers, and the whole work of nature in thy vast creation. Grant us grace to give glory to thee also with our lives, that our lives and lips may agree in praise and devotion to thee, after the pattern of thy Son, even Jesus Christ our Lord.   Amen.   (103)

143   Praise for Freedom of Worship

Almighty God, who art high and lifted up, and who art blessed, good, gracious, and merciful, we rejoice that we may bow before thee in adoration and petition, for thou art ever willing to hear us. Accept our heartfelt thanks for the privilege of worshiping thee and approaching thy throne of grace with all our needs. Help us to promote the faithful use of the freedom we have to worship thee. Through Jesus Christ our Lord, we pray.   Amen.   (103)

144   A Prayer of Chrysostom

Almighty God, who hast given us grace at this time with one accord to make our common supplications unto thee, and dost promise that where two or three are gathered together in thy name thou wilt grant their requests, fulfill now, O Lord, the desires and petitions of thy servants, as may be most expedient for them, granting us in this world knowledge of thy truth, and in the world to come life everlasting.   Amen.   (66)

145   Litany Based on a Prayer by Francis of Assisi
(to be read responsively; dashes indicate pauses)
Lord, make me an instrument of thy peace————

An instrument, Lord————

A worker for peace————

That peace which is not a narcotic to lull us into indifference or lethargy————

That peace which is not a false hope in an idle illusion of the placid life————

But that peace which disturbs and moves, which struggles and perspires, which works and wrestles.

Where there is hate, may I bring love————

An instrument, Lord————

A worker for love————

Love that is not blind to the fierce reality of hate————

Love that is not vapid sentimentality but the deeper burden of concern————

Love which is forbearing and kind. Love which knows no jealousy. Love which does not brag, is not conceited. Love which is not unmannerly, nor selfish, nor irritable, nor mindful of wrongs. Love which does not rejoice in injustice, but joyfully sides with the truth. Love which can overlook faults, which is full of trust, of hope, of endurance.

Where offense, may I bring pardon————

An instrument, Lord————

A worker for pardon————

Not that I might offer my forgiveness alone————but that I may be the channel through which the greater pardon and acceptance flow.

May I bring union in the place of discord————

The shattered and scattered fragments of nations and races, of families, and men lie about me————

The cry for wholeness dins upon my ears————

How shall I answer, Lord?————

Proclaiming good news to the poor————to those who are deprived of wholeness.

Announcing release to those whose lives are bound in chains.

Giving sight to the sightless and the insightless.

Freeing those whom tyranny has crushed.

May I bring faith, where once there was doubt———
Faith whose foundation is composed of rubble, once the house of doubt———
Faith the armor, not the escape———
Faith the challenge to life, the strength of living.
May I give hope for despair, light for darkness, joy for sadness———
Blind me not to the reality of despair, of darkness, of sadness———
Yet, open my eyes to the seed of hope which can grow from despair ———the ray of light that glimmers in the darkness———the joy that comes from victory in sadness.
Teach me, Lord, to add to my need for love, a need to love others———
Willing to give love, without seeking love in return———
Yet, knowing that as I am loved by thee, so can I love———
Help me, Lord, to learn that in giving I may receive———
Receiving I would not despise, for from it I get to give———
Truly giving has its foundations in receiving, as receiving rests upon the giving.
In forgetting self, may I find life eternal———
My selfishness I would forget———
My true self I would forget not, but find in thee.   Amen.   *Amen.*
(50)

146   Direct Us

Direct us, O Lord, in all our doings with thy most gracious favor, and further us with thy continual help; that in all our works, begun, continued, and ended in thee, we may glorify thy holy name, and finally, by thy mercy, obtain everlasting life; through Jesus Christ our Lord.   Amen.   (38)

147   For the Coming Days

For the coming days cause thy grace, O almighty God, to triumph over our infirmities and grant us inwardly such increased steadfastness and in our lives such a larger harvest of good that through sunshine and storm we may trust and not be afraid, work and not be weary, suffer and not complain, overcome all evils with patience; and in humility and peace possess our souls in full assurance of righteousness and sanctification and wisdom.

To thee, most gracious Father, we dedicate ourselves and all that we have, beseeching thee to guide our hands, our minds, and our whole energies to those things which are worthy of ourselves and pleasing to thee. Through Jesus Christ our Lord, we pray. Amen.

(22)

148 For the Kingdom

Lord God, heavenly Father, we are assembled in thy name to consider the work of thy kingdom. We thank thee that thou hast called us into thy church and committed unto us the task of cooperating with thee in bringing thy kingdom on earth. Make each of us conscious of thy presence. Help us to think thy thoughts after thee. Help us to decide what is right and give us then the courage to execute those decisions to thy name's glory and thy people's good. In the name of thy Son, Jesus our Lord, we pray. Amen. (18)

149 For Parents and Teachers

Divine Instructor, melt us together as parents and teachers into a common mold of concern—that of nurturing children in the admonition of the Lord. Remind us that such guardianship is little lower than that of the angels. Enlighten us so that we rightly fashion the hearts and quicken the pulses of the young. Lead us daily to Calvary so that there, caught up by the spell of thy love, we will be enabled to draw the violin bow of thy compassion across the restless heartstrings of our youth and set their lives in tune with thee.

Draw us all with magnetic spirit about the Cross and write upon the easel of our hearts, "The fear of the Lord is the beginning of wisdom."

And, finally, mount us as fit jewels for thy heavenly crown. To that end, commission us ever to go before men as sermons walking. In Jesus' name, we pray. Amen. (63)

150   Supply All Our Needs

O God, most holy, wise, and powerful preserver and governor of all
thy creatures and all their actions, keep us, we beseech thee, in health
of body and soundness of mind, in purity of heart and cheerfulness
of spirit, in contentment with our lot and charity with our neighbor; and further all our lawful undertakings with thy blessing. In our
labor strengthen us; in our pleasure purify us; in our difficulties direct us; in our perils defend us; in our troubles comfort us; and
supply all our needs according to the riches of thy grace in Christ
Jesus our Lord.   Amen.   (135)

Dedication of a Home

151   For a New Home

O gracious Father, who through thy Son didst find fellowship in the
homes of friends, enter, we pray, and be a constant guest in this our
home. May the radiance of thy presence be felt here at all times so
that all who enter or dwell here may find strength, solace, rest,
relaxation, peace, and joy, and be enabled to exclaim with Jacob
of old, "Surely the Lord is in this place." This we ask in the name of
our blessed Christ.   Amen.   (62)

152   Prayer for the Dedication of a Home

O God, our heavenly Father, giver and sustainer of life, let thy
beauty be upon this new home which we dedicate to thee. Let all
hindrances to godly living be driven from it, and all that is pure,
tender, and true find fruition under its shelter. In the name of thy
Son, our Savior, we pray.   Amen.   (89)

Intercessions

153   A Prayer of Concern for Others

O God our Father, whose Son looked upon the multitudes and was moved with compassion for them because they were distressed and scattered as sheep having no shepherd, grant us some measure of his love and concern for all who specially need thy help. Give to those who grieve the comfort of thy grace and hope, to those in perplexity the leadings of thy Holy Spirit, thy strength to those who are fighting hard battles or are called upon to make difficult decisions, thy peace and power to those in trouble and anxiety. And bind us all together in the bonds of sympathy and faith. We pray in the name of him who is touched with the feeling of our infirmities since he was tempted in all points as we are, even Jesus Christ our Lord and Savior.   Amen.   (138)

154   For the Needs of Men

We pray, O heavenly Father, for thy church; awaken her heart. May the church go forth to win mankind unto thee. Empower her life by thy Holy Spirit. Keep her ever mindful of the needs of men and of the redemptive mission of thy Son, our Savior.

Through the church help men and women to find grace for every trial, comfort in the time of grief, and strength for every time of temptation.   Amen.   (143)

155   Strength Through Inner Peace

Be still—be still—be still and know that I am God. O Father, we would realize ever more fully that in quietness and confidence shall be our strength. Cause our hearts to be truly quiet, so that thy peace may enter in. And as we wait before thee, speak to us through thy Word and Spirit the message that gives us guidance and support for whatever tasks thou hast for us today.   Amen.   (142)

✳

For the Sick and the Distressed

156   For the Ill

We beseech thee to comfort those who are ill. By the knowledge that all things work together for good to those who love thee, assure them that thou wilt enable them to await thy healing with patience; thy peace with hope; thy house of many mansions with faith. Through Jesus Christ our Lord, we pray.   Amen.   (103)

157   For Times of Distress

Almighty God and Father, we are assured thou art nearer than breathing, closer than life itself. Yet we acknowledge humbly and penitently that we too often allow sickness and distress of body, mind, or spirit, to make us forget this assurance. Help each of us to realize that while thou never causest evil or trouble, yet thou hast frequently used evil—even the evil of crucifixion—to further thy eternal plan.

O God, bring not only this realization to our own consciousness, but help us convey this eternal hope to those we know who are sorely beset with the trials and afflictions of life. So many times we have seen thee use these distressing circumstances to make mediocre people good, and good people great, that we would transmit this gospel truth to all who need it to sustain, to maintain life itself.

We pray in the name of Jesus Christ, who himself always turned the bitterest of events into triumphantly glorious proclamations of thy unsurpassed love and concern for us.   Amen.   (48)

158   For the Sick

Eternal God, who carest for all, remember in thy mercy those who are sick; assure them of thy love and help. Bless the means that are being used for their recovery. And give unto them the peace which passes all understanding, guarding their hearts and minds in Christ Jesus our Lord.   Amen.   (102)

159   Intercession

Eternal Father in heaven, in whose hands our lives are held, we thank thee that we may cast our cares upon thee, and that thou carest for each of us, even as a shepherd cares for his sheep. Be with [name] and assure him (or her) that nothing shall ever separate him (or her) from thy love. Bless the means that are being used for his (or her) health, and continue thy gracious work, that all things may work together for good. Through Jesus Christ our Lord, we pray.   Amen.

(102)

160   A Prayer for Healing

Thou divine source of all life and healing, our heavenly Father, we turn to thee in our prayers. Humbly we beseech thee, deem us worthy, through the grace of our Lord Jesus, to receive the healing virtues of thy redeeming love in body, soul, and mind. Thou, our Savior, art the great physician who didst go about doing good and healing all manner of diseases. Continue thy gracious work among us. We pray for those who are sick, remembering them now by face or name. Grant unto them patience in waiting, faith in thy boundless love, courage to look ahead to brighter days, and deliverance from pain and suffering. Comfort and guide us with thy Presence and we shall always praise thee for the healing power of thy divine love.   Amen.

(112)

In the Valley of Shadows

161   When a Loved One Is Called Home

Thou, O Father, hast assured us, "Though my father and my mother forsake me, the Lord will take me up." Even though our family ties are precious, more precious is the bond that unites us to thee, the unchangeable one, our all-loving Father. Into thy hands we commit our loved one knowing that there he is provided for and blessed

beyond what eye hath seen and ear hath heard. Strengthen us in the
faith that living or dying, we are thine and hence are never beyond
thy loving care.   Amen.   (142)

162   Prayer for Those Who Mourn

Merciful Father, whose promises to sustain the suffering and to bind
up the brokenhearted are most surely true, enable us to turn to thee
in time of sorrow. When the chill of bereavement enwraps our
hearts, help us to know that thou dost understand our pain and
grief, our sorrow for loss, our inability to comprehend the ways of
life and death. Bless those who mourn; in their mourning may they
find comfort. May we as members of the Christian fellowship of the
concerned be instruments of thy healing love as we seek to minister
to the grief-stricken with the warm handclasp of Christian friendship, the sympathetic and understanding word, and the sharing of
their burdens. In the name of him who brought comfort to all men,
we pray.   Amen.   (50)

163   In a National Crisis

King of kings and Lord of lords, thou Lord of life and death, protect our nation in its great need. Let men use this trial to turn to
thee for strength and to find in Jesus their peace with thee. Let wise
counsel, calm thinking, unselfish aims prevail. Grant unity to the
land and support of all just measures. In Jesus' name, we pray.
Amen.   (69)

164   For Divine Support at the Last

O Lord, support us all the day long of this troublous life, until the
shadows lengthen and the evening comes, and the busy world is
hushed, and the fever of life is over, and our work is done. Then in
thy great mercy grant us a safe lodging, a holy rest, and peace at the
last; through Jesus Christ our Lord.   Amen.   (84)

❋

Closing Prayers

165   Meditation on the Lord's Prayer

Our Father, who art in heaven—God of love and of might;
Hallowed be thy name—we look up to thee in reverence.
Thy kingdom come—we look out to all thy world.
Thy will be done on earth as in heaven—we look within our lives
to thy help.
Give us this day our daily bread—we pray for the needs of today.
Forgive us our debts, as we forgive our debtors—we pray for the
needs of yesterday, of all our yesterdays.
Lead us not into temptation, but deliver us from evil—we pray
for help tomorrow, and for all our tomorrows.
For thine is the kingdom and the power and the glory, forever—we
leave it all in thy hands.   Amen.   (82)

166   To Follow Thy Leadings

Spirit of God, like a flame of fire, we thank thee for the love kindled
amongst us by thy presence. Warm our lives in the brotherhood of
faith, ever to be sensitive to thy leadings and able to respond obediently. Shine through the darkness to guide us on our ways. Ever be
thou our light in whom is no shadow nor turning. For Jesus' sake,
we pray.   Amen.   (55)

167   Guide Us as We Part

Gracious God, our only fountain of wisdom and source of power, we
give thanks to thee that thou hast been with us during these rich
moments we have spent together in fellowship with one another and
with thee. As we leave this meeting, we pray that thou wouldst bless
whatever we have said and done that was in harmony with thy will,
and bring to naught whatever was not good in thy sight. Keep us in
thy way, while we are absent from one another, that not one of us
may stray away from thy paths. Help us to accomplish the work thou

hast given us to do, and may thy peace dwell in our hearts richly, now, and evermore.   Amen.   (34)

168   Strengthen Us
Dear Lord, we see that our tasks are much too big for us alone. But we are not alone. Thou art with us. Our sufficiency is of thee. And thou art great beyond any demand that is upon us now, or ever can be. Help us then in thy strength to go forward bravely and do our duty gladly. We ask it in Jesus' name.   Amen.   (34)

169   In Closing We Thank Thee
Almighty God, our heavenly Father, we praise thy holy name! We thank thee for all that thou hast done, and for all thou art doing. Strengthen us to do thy will. Forgive us whenever we have failed to please thee. Help us day by day, and bless us in every way; and we shall praise thee for all thy benefits.   Amen.   (102)

Offertory Sentences

170   Matthew 5:16
Let your light so shine before men, that they may see your good works and give glory to your Father who is in heaven.

171   Acts 20:35
In all things I have shown you that by so toiling one must help the weak, remembering the words of the Lord Jesus, how he said, "It is more blessed to give than to receive."

172   2 Corinthians 9:6-7
The point is this: he who sows sparingly will also reap sparingly, and he who sows bountifully will also reap bountifully. Each one

must do as he has made up his mind, not reluctantly or under compulsion, for God loves a cheerful giver.

173   What We Share
Not what we give, but what we share,
For the gift without the giver is bare;
Who gives himself with his alms feeds three—
Himself, his hungering neighbor, and me.   (67)

Offertory Prayers[1]

174   The Love of Thankful Hearts
Gracious Lord, with every breath we give thee thanks for life, energy, and hope. All that we have we receive from thee each day. Accept, we pray, these offerings from the sweat of toil, the care of mind, and the love of thankful hearts, that they may serve Christ.   Amen.
(55)

175   Treasures in Heaven
O God, who dost bid us to work while it is day, before the night comes when no man can work, accept these gifts which we offer in grateful memory of the supreme sacrifice of thy Son. Help us to lay up treasures for ourselves in heaven. In Jesus' name, we pray. Amen.   (103)

[1] Responses such as "We Give Thee but Thine Own" or "Bless Thou the Gifts Our Hands Have Brought" may be used.

Welcome to Visitors and New Members

176   Various Ways of Expressing a Welcome to Visitors

1. We extend a cordial welcome to visitors among us. May we all find inspiration and strength for daily tasks and duties as we join in the activities of the church.

2. We give a hearty welcome and sincere greeting to all who are with us. On behalf of our members, we would especially greet our visitors and invite them to all the activities of our church.

3. To all who desire to learn of him who is the way, the truth, and the life, the organizations of this church bid a cordial welcome. May every visitor find this to be a house of prayer where we are all guests of God and fellow workers.   (102)

**177   A Brief Form for the Organizational Reception of
        New Members**

(The president or installing officer may pronounce the name or names of the new members and ask such present to appear before him at the front of the room, where he may say:)

Dear Friend (s):

The object of our organization is to worship God, study his Word, serve his cause, and enjoy the fellowship of his children. The church needs people who unselfishly and sacrificially give time, talents, and substance in joyful service to our God. Therefore we are happy to know that you have decided to become *a member* (members) of [name of organization].

(A few words may be spoken here, if desired, about the organization and how it undergirds the entire program of the church. A copy of some pertinent literature may be given with appropriate words.)

It is expected by those who unite with this fellowship that they will not only share in its privileges, but that they will also help to fulfill its objectives. By word and deed, the beauty and power of the Christian life will be made manifest.

Since you are now about to be received into the [name of organization], I ask you in the presence of God and this group: Do you promise that you will seek, with the help of God, to lead a truly Christian life; that you will cooperate with the decisions of this organization, and that you will promote the welfare and projects of [name of organization] according to your ability? Then answer: I do.

Answer: *I do.*

On behalf of the officers and the other members of our [name of organization], I extend to you a cordial welcome and give you the right hand of fellowship. Your willingness to work with us will be encouraging to us, and we trust that our cooperative spirit will be evident to you as well.

Let us bow our heads for prayer:

Almighty God, the Father of our Lord Jesus Christ and through him our heavenly Father, we thank thee for the fellowship we have with one another and with thee. We praise thee for the power thou dost give to thy disciples. We rejoice in the opportunities for service which are open to us. Bless our [name of organization], our new member (s), and our purposes. Strengthen us all in the might of thy Holy Spirit. Through Jesus Christ our Lord, we pray.   Amen. (102)

Table Prayers

178   Gratitude for Fulfilling Our Needs

We thank thee, O Lord, that in thy great love thou hast made provision for the bodily needs of all thy children. Accept also our thanks for the opportunity of fellowship which thou dost at this time offer unto us. May thy Son be the unseen guest at our table.   Amen.   (3)

179   Bless Our Fellowship

Almighty God, creator of all things visible and invisible, giver of things temporal and eternal, bless our fellowship as well as these gifts which have been prepared from thy bounty, for our nourishment and the upbuilding of the finer life; for Jesus' sake. Amen.

(102)

180   Strengthen and Refresh Us

O Lord God of heaven and earth, who providest from the riches of thy bounty for our daily needs, we thank thee for the provisions which are set before us. Strengthen and refresh us, and bless our fellowship with one another around these tables. Through Jesus Christ our Lord, we pray.   Amen.   (102)

181   It Is Good to Give Thanks

It is good to give thanks to the Lord, to sing praises to thy name, O Most High; to declare thy steadfast love in the morning, and thy faithfulness by night.

We give thanks to thee, O Lord, for thou art good; and thy steadfast love endures forever.   Amen.

182   Thanks for Spiritual Food

O thou who didst feed the multitude upon the hillside, so feed us now with this bread set before us and with the spiritual bread which thou art ever ready to share with him who looks to thee in faith. Amen.

(3)

183   A Child Gives Thanks

Dear God, we thank you for this food,
For rest and home and all things good,
For wind and rain and sun above,
But most of all for those we love.   Amen.   (134)

5
Devotional Aids for the Church Year

❄

Advent

ADVENT LIGHTS (For the four Sundays before Christmas)

ON the first Sunday in Advent, place a large unlighted candle on one corner of a table. Light it during the course of your worship program. On the second Sunday light the candle before your devotions begin; place a second candle on another corner of the table and light that candle during the course of your second worship program. On the third Sunday, start with two lighted candles and light a third; on the fourth Sunday, start with three lighted candles and light a fourth.

There are many good Advent hymns. Learning a few of those that are not so well known could add to the interest and value of your Advent devotions. You may wish to have your group read a hymn together instead of, or in addition to, singing it. Hymns have much to teach us about the meaning of Advent. It is hardly necessary to say that Christmas carols may also be used, especially as the season draws closer to December 25.

Suggestions for hymns, scripture readings, and prayers for use during the four Sundays in Advent are given below.

First Sunday

Hymns: "Watchman, Tell Us of the Night," "Come, Thou Long-expected Jesus," "Arise, the Kingdom Is at Hand."

*When the scripture reading, such as Isaiah 41:1-10 or Isaiah 1:1-20
has been finished, the reader or some designated person lights the
first Advent light. As he does so, he says:*

"Prepare the way of the Lord, make straight in the desert a highway for our God. . . . The glory of the Lord shall be revealed, and all
flesh shall see it together."

184　　Help Us to Receive His Blessing

Almighty God, who in thy wise providence hast made all ages to be
the highway for the coming of thy Son, we pray that thou wilt prepare our hearts to receive the blessing of his presence, promised to all
who sincerely gather in his name. Make thyself known to us on this
day in Advent. Open the eyes of our understanding, that we may
grow in the grace and knowledge of him who came to bring us life,
and that more abundantly.　Amen.　　　　　　　　　　　　　(79)

185　　Fill Us

Lord Jesus, open wide the window of our spirits, and fill us full of
light; open wide the door of our hearts, that we may receive and en-
tertain thee with all our powers of adoration and love.　Amen.　(16)

Second Sunday

Hymns: "Lift Up Your Heads, Ye Mighty Gates," "Rejoice, Rejoice,
Believers," "On Jordan's Bank the Baptist's Cry."

*After the scripture lesson, which may have consisted of Isaiah 9:1-6
or Isaiah 2:1-17 or Isaiah 5:1-16, the reader or some designated person lights the second Advent light. As he does so, he says:*

"To us a child is born, to us a son is given . . . and his name will
be called 'Wonderful Counselor, Mighty God, Everlasting Father,
Prince of Peace.'"

186　　For the Indwelling Christ

O God, who didst prepare of old the minds and hearts of men for
the coming of thy Son, and whose spirit ever worketh to illumine our
darkened lives with the light of the gospel, prepare now our minds

and hearts, we beseech thee, that Christ may dwell within us, and ever reign in our thoughts and affections as the King of Love and the Prince of Peace. Grant this, we pray thee, for his sake. Amen.

(115)

187 For Thy Spirit Among the Nations

O God, for whose spirit our world hungers and thirsts, bless us with peace and righteousness the world over as the season of good will comes upon us. Let thy spirit rule among the nations, that concord and mutual service may be established, and that the mind of Christ may bind people with people and race with race in brotherhood.

Support all those at this season who think and plan to give happiness to others, and give them the deepest joy in their tasks. Sustain all those who must bear added burdens to provide cheer for others. Help us all to be mindful and considerate of them. . . . Abundantly bless those in whose hearts there is little room for joy because sorrow has come to them. Grant that in the knowledge of Christ's comfort they may find the peace that knows no end. Amen.

(86)

Third Sunday

Hymns: "O'er the Distant Mountains Breaking," "Lo! He Comes with Clouds Descending," "Wake, Awake, for Night Is Flying."

After the scripture lesson, such as Luke 1:46-55, Isaiah 12, or Isaiah 55, the reader or some designated person lights the third Advent light. As he does so, he says:

"My soul magnifies the Lord, and my spirit rejoices in God my Savior . . . for he who is mighty has done great things for me, and holy is his name."

188 Deepen Our Faith

Almighty God, give us grace that we may cast away the works of darkness, and put upon us the armor of light now in the time of this mortal life, in which thy Son Jesus Christ came to visit us in great humility. Awaken us from our slumbers. Quicken us, O thou who art eternal life. Revive and deepen our faith in spiritual realities. Kindle our affections and restore us to hope. Our eyes wait for the glorious and blessed dawn. Let us behold that dayspring from on high that we may live in peace, and depart in peace.   Amen.   (48)

189   For the Brightness of Thy Glory

O God, the Father of our Lord Jesus Christ, who by thy providence hast made all ages a preparation for the coming of thy dear Son, make ready our hearts, we beseech thee, for the brightness of thy glory, and fill them with the power of thy divine presence. Through Jesus Christ our Lord, we pray.   Amen.   (128)

Fourth Sunday

Hymns: "Hail to the Lord's Anointed," "O Come, O Come, Emmanuel," "O How Shall I Receive Thee"

After reading Luke 1:68-79, Isaiah 42, Jeremiah 23, or Isaiah 11:1-6, 9 as the scripture lesson, the reader or some person appointed lights the fourth Advent light. As he does so, he says:

"Blessed be the Lord God of Israel, for he has visited and redeemed his people. . . . The day shall dawn upon us from on high to give light to those who sit in darkness and in the shadow of death, to guide our feet into the way of peace."

190   Help Us to Find Thee

Eternal Father, as we worship in thy house, prepare us to rejoice as the shepherds rejoiced at the sound of the angels' song. Fill us with joy as we hear again the story of thy love. As the Wise Men brought their gifts to the Christchild, help us to bring the richest treasures of our devotion and lay them before thy majesty. As seekers in the past followed the star that led them to the shrine of his birth, prepare our hearts for the fulfillment of our need, that in this hour of worship we may find thee, and be led to life eternal. Through Jesus Christ our Lord, we pray.   Amen.   (80)

191   A Penitential Psalm (Psalm 51 ad)

Have mercy on us, O God, according to thy steadfast love; according to thy abundant mercy blot out our transgressions. Wash us thoroughly from our iniquities and cleanse us from our sin. For we know our transgressions, and our sin is ever before us. Purge us, and we shall be clean; wash us, and we shall be whiter than snow. Create in us clean hearts, O God, and put a right spirit within us. Cast us not away from thy presence, and take not thy Holy Spirit from us. Amen.

ADDITIONAL WORSHIP AIDS

192   Help Us to Seek

O God, who hast promised to be an everlasting light to thy people, hasten the day, we beseech thee, when all people will prepare for thy coming, and seek for satisfaction on the high levels of life, that they may rejoice in thy wonderful glory and grace in the face of Jesus Christ.   Amen.   (102)

193   For Good Will

O God of kindness and beauty, who didst reveal thyself in Jesus Christ, we give thee our hearty and humble thanks for his coming. In this season of preparation for the coming of the King, mercifully grant that our hearts may be filled with the spirit of good will, that peace and brotherhood may cover the earth. In the name of the Prince of Peace, we pray.   Amen.   (102)

194   An Advent Collect

O Lord, we beseech thee, mercifully to hear the prayers of thy people, that we, who for our sins are justly afflicted, may be consoled by thy visitation; who livest and reignest with the Father and the Holy Spirit, ever one God, world without end.   Amen.   (24)

195   An Advent Prayer Using the Hymn "Thou Didst Leave Thy Throne"

> Thou didst leave thy throne
> And thy kingly crown,
> When thou camest to earth for me;
> But in Bethlehem's home

There was found no room
For thy holy nativity.
O come to my heart, Lord Jesus,
There is room in my heart for thee.

Yes, Lord, we need and long for thy coming to bring the hope of
salvation to thy people now, as of long ago. We are poor and needy,
our hearts are unclean and ill prepared for thy holy advent.

Send out thy light and thy truth, let them lead us to thy holy hill
and to thy tabernacle. Help us to stand before thee in deep humility
and sincere expectation of thy appearance to take full possession of
our lives. Wash the windows of our souls with the cleansing water
of repentance so that we may behold thee with the eyes of faith and
accept thee as our King of Glory.

Come thou blessed hope of every nation,
Our soul's delight and stay

make our heart to be thy dwelling place, be our honored guest, Savior
and Lord, now and forever. Hear and bless us for thy dear name's
sake.   Amen.   (41)

Christmastide

CHRISTMAS DEVOTIONS

Prelude or a Medley of Christmas Carols

196   Opening Sentences: Isaiah 9:2, 6
The people who walked in darkness
Have seen a great light;
Those who dwell in a land of deep darkness,
On them has light shined.
For to us a child is born,
To us a son is given;
(All) And the government will be upon his shoulder,

And his name will be called
"Wonderful Counselor, Mighty God,
Everlasting Father, Prince of Peace."

Hymn: "O Come, All Ye Faithful," or "Hark, the Herald Angels Sing"

197   Prayer of Adoration
Gracious God, who didst wonderfully bless us through thy Son who was born in Bethlehem, we glorify thee and praise thee for thy unspeakable gift for the whole world. Wherefore we come to adore him who is Christ the Lord.   Amen.   (102)

Hymn: "Joy to the World" or "It Came upon the Midnight Clear"

Leader: Let us humbly confess our sins unto almighty God:

198   Confession of Sins
Almighty and all-holy Father, we confess ourselves unworthy of thine unspeakable gift. We have not loved thee as we ought; nor have we always been loving to one another, kindhearted, forgiving one another, even as thou, for Christ's sake, hast forgiven us. We have lived in selfishness and worldly pride, and the good gifts thou hast bestowed upon us we have not used to relieve the burdens of others. Pardon and blot out our offenses, we beseech thee, through the incarnate life and willing sacrifice of thy holy Son, even Jesus Christ our Lord.   Amen.   (127)

(Or the following confession)

199   Confession of Sins
We rejoice this day in the unquenchable and eternal light that lighteth every man that cometh into the world. In that light we are ashamed of those greeds within us that have darkened our own souls, and those selfish customs among us that have shadowed the lives and spirits of others. We seek thy presence here, O thou Most High, not alone for our joy today, but to illumine the ways of all our doings until every child of man shall be brought out of darkness into thy marvelous light.   Amen.   (137)

200　　Assurance of Pardon

God so loved the world that he gave his only Son, that whoever believes in him should not perish but have eternal life.

Hear the gracious words of our Lord Jesus Christ for all who truly repent and turn to him:

Come to me, all who labor and are heavy-laden, and I will give you rest.

The grace of our Lord Jesus Christ be with you all.　Amen.

First Scripture Lesson: Luke 2:1-20.

Hymn: "Silent Night! Holy Night!" or "O Little Town of Bethlehem"

Second Scripture Lesson: John 1:1-14, or Matthew 2:1-12.

201　　A Confession of Faith

I believe that Jesus Christ—true God, begotten of the Father from eternity, and also true man, born of the Virgin Mary—is my Lord.　　　　　　　　　　　　　　　　　　　　　　　　(71)

202　　A Prayer for the Gift of Charity

Almighty God, who by the birth of thy holy child Jesus hast given us a great light to dawn upon our darkness, grant, we pray thee, that in his light we may see light to the end of our days; and bestow upon us, we beseech thee, that most excellent Christmas gift of charity to all men, that the likeness of thy Son may be formed in us, and that we may have the ever-brightening hope of everlasting life. Through Jesus Christ our Lord, we pray.　Amen.　　　　　　　　(58)

203　　A Prayer for Good Will

O God our Father, who didst send forth thy Son to be King of kings and Prince of Peace, grant that all the kingdoms of this world may become the kingdom of Christ, and that they may learn of him the way of peace. Send forth among all men the spirit of good will and reconciliation. Let those who are offended forgive, and those who have offended repent, so that all thy children may live together as one family, praising thee and blessing thee for the great redemption which thou hast wrought for us. Through Jesus Christ our Lord, we pray. Amen. (92)

204 Benediction (Numbers 6:24-26 ad)
The Lord bless us, and keep us:
The Lord make his face to shine upon us, and be gracious to us:
(All) The Lord lift up his countenance upon us, and give us peace.
Amen.

ADDITIONAL WORSHIP AIDS

205 Call to Worship
O come, let us keep Christmas
And oft the good news tell
That Jesus Christ is born tonight
And in our hearts would dwell.
O listen to the story
Of love made known to men
And plan through every single day
To make it live again. (74)

206 An Act of Intercession and Supplication *(to be read responsively)*
Let us pray for others as well as for ourselves as we approach the throne of grace:
For all who have come to celebrate Christmas with their families,
We thank thee, O God.
For all who have responsibilities in establishing peace and good will among men, and especially for the leaders of the nations and the United Nations,
We beseech thee to hear us, good Lord.
For each one of us, that the Christmas joy and peace may bring us closer to him,

We implore thy blessings.

(All) Help us, like Mary, to keep his sayings and ponder them in our hearts. Amen. (102)

207   Help Us to Celebrate His Birth

Help all thy children, almighty and eternal God, to celebrate the memory of Jesus' birth in the right spirit. Enable us to look to Jesus with true faith and joy; to love him as did Mary; and to worship and honor him daily. Give us grace to grow in his knowledge and cause us to serve him faithfully every day of the year.   Amen.   (30 ad)

208   A Christmas Prayer

Dear God, we thank thee for the joy and warmth of this Christmas season. Help us to remember and share with people the world around who are hungry, friendless, and lonely. We thank thee for those people who have shared with us their carols and beautiful Christmas customs that make our Christmas more meaningful. So fill us with the spirit of love that we may feel the real glow of a Christian Christmas. In Jesus' name, we pray.   Amen.   (53)

209   An Offertory Prayer for Christmas

O great Giver of all good and perfect gifts, who hast given us thy Son Jesus Christ as a babe in Bethlehem for our enlightenment and salvation, accept these tokens of our love for thee and thy Son. For his sake, we pray.   Amen.   (103)

210   A New Christmas Blessing

> May the hope and peace of Christmas
> Bring you happiness today
> And his love be with you always
> As you follow in his way. (42)

A member of a Youth Fellowship who was requested to give her reactions to these worship aids asked, "Would it be possible to suggest a nativity scene with a few members re-enacting the Christmas story while it is being read? Or does that require too much work on the part of the youth group?" Then she went on to say, "It could be done quite simply and yet beautifully."

Some Christmas stories are *Why the Chimes Rang* by Raymond M. Alden; *The Birds' Christmas Carol* by Kate D. Wiggins; *Christmas Carol* by Charles Dickens; *A Tree for Peter* by Kate Seredy; *Christmas Everywhere* by Elizabeth H. Sechrist; *This Way to Christmas* by Ruth Sawyer; "The Legend of the Black Madonna" from *The Merry-Go-Round* by Margaret T. Applegarth. *Let's Keep Christmas* by Peter Marshall may also be considered for reading or re-telling.

Epiphany

THESE devotions are for January 6 and any of the following days in the church season of Epiphany.

211 Lead Us to Thy Will
Almighty and all-merciful God, help the church of Christ throughout the world to rise to the meanings of thy purpose which beat like wings about thy throne. Lead us from height to height, from vision to vision, from truth to truth, until at last we enter into that broad place where thy purpose shall be our purpose, and thy will, our will. Amen. (4)

212 For Faith to Endure
O God, who dost govern all things in heaven and on earth, grant us grace, we beseech thee, to look beyond the things which are seen and temporal to the things which are unseen and eternal; that walking by faith, we may not be unduly moved by circumstances in this world, but be able to endure to the end in the way of life. Through Jesus Christ our Lord, we pray. Amen. (128)

213   A Collect for Transfiguration Sunday[1]

O God, who by thy Son Jesus Christ hast made the world to shine with the brightness of the true light, grant that we who have now come to know thee here by faith, may be conducted to the full vision of thy glory hereafter in heaven. Through Jesus Christ our Lord, we pray. Amen.   (128)

✳

Lent

DEVOTIONS IN LENT
The devotions that follow may be used during Lent on one of the forty-six days before Easter.

Prelude

Hymn: "When I Survey the Wondrous Cross" or "O Come and Mourn with Me Awhile" or "In the Cross of Christ I Glory"

214   Opening Sentences (Matthew 16:24-25; *to be read responsively*)
Then Jesus told his disciples, "If any man would come after me, let him deny himself and take up his cross and follow me.
   For whoever would save his life will lose it, and whoever loses his life for my sake will find it."
   (All sing or say the words of the hymn):
                        Jesus calls us: o'er the tumult
                           Of our life's wild, restless sea,
                        Day by day his sweet voice soundeth,
                           Saying, "Christian, follow me."

---

[1] The transfiguration is generally observed the last Sunday after the Epiphany, unless it is observed on August 6.

215   Call to Confession (2 Chronicles 7:14)

If my people who are called by my name humble themselves, and pray and seek my face, and turn from their wicked ways, then I will hear from heaven, and will forgive their sin.

216   Confession of Sins (Psalm 25:6-7; *to be read responsively*)

Be mindful of thy mercy, O Lord, and of thy steadfast love, for they have been from of old.

Remember not the sins of my youth, or my transgressions;
According to thy steadfast love remember me,
For thy goodness' sake, O Lord!

217   Words of Challenge and Assurance (Ephesians 4:32)

Be kind to one another, tenderhearted, forgiving one another, as God in Christ forgave you.

218   Corporate Prayer *(to be read responsively)*

O God the Father, who knowest our necessities,
Hear us, thy servants.
O God the Son, who was tempted like as we are,
Hear us, thy servants.
O God the Holy Spirit, who knowest how to deliver the godly out of temptation,
Hear us, thy servants.
O Lord God, we pray thee to make us know ourselves as thou knowest us, and to see our sins as thou seest them.
Help us to set our minds more on thee and less on the world.
Help us to resist the devil, as good soldiers of Jesus Christ.
Help us to keep our thoughts pure, our words holy, and our bodies chaste as temples of thy Holy Spirit.
Lead us to give up something for thee.
Lead us to help some person in body or soul.
Lead us to pray for thy holy church.
Make us obey thee as thy children.
Make us love thee as members of Christ.

Make us serve thee as inheritors of the kingdom of heaven.

ALL: *Grant us so to take up our cross daily here, that we may receive the crown of glory hereafter. Through Jesus Christ our Lord, we pray. Amen.*   (36 ad)

First Scripture Lesson—Jesus on Trial: Matthew 27:1-31 or Mark 15:1-20 or Luke 23:1-25 or John 18:12-27; 18:28—19:16
   (If the passages from the Gospel According to John are chosen, they may be read by two persons.)

Hymn: "Go to Dark Gethsemane" or "In the Hour of Trial" or "Jesus, Refuge of the Weary"

Second Scripture Lesson—The Crucifixion and Death of Jesus Christ: Matthew 27:32-66 or Mark 15:21-47 or Luke 23:26-56 or John 19:17-37

Hymn: "O Sacred Head, Now Wounded" or "Jesus, We Adore Thee" or "Beneath the Cross of Jesus" or "Alas! And Did my Savior Bleed"

The Lord's Prayer

A Moment of Silence

Benediction: *May the peace of God, which passes all understanding, keep our hearts and minds through Christ Jesus. Amen.*

ADDITIONAL WORSHIP AIDS

219   Invocation
O God, who through the Cross hast shown us the greatness of thy love, grant that by it we may be led to see what has enduring value, that we may devote ourselves only to that which is pleasing to thee, and thus gain life everlasting. Through Jesus Christ our Lord, we pray.   Amen.   (145)

220   Palm Sunday Invocation
O Lord Jesus Christ, our Savior King, who didst humbly enter the Holy City while people sang thy praises, come into our hearts and

master us that we may openly love thee and obediently follow thee. Lift us, through the inspiration of all that is high and holy, that we may joyfully praise thee now and all the days of our life; and we shall magnify thy name together with that of the Father and the Holy Spirit, world without end. Amen. (102)

221 Invocation for Maundy Thursday
O Lord Jesus Christ, who on the night of thy betrayal didst bless us more than we can say, bestow upon us the spirit of humility and grateful obedience to thy will. Cleanse us from all sin and renew a right spirit within us. Through the message in word and song and sacrament, bind us in living fellowship with thee, now and forever. Amen. (102)

222 Invocation for Good Friday, or for Another Day in Lent
O Lord Jesus Christ, our Savior, who didst come into the world to save sinners, we humbly praise and thank thee for bearing our griefs and carrying our sorrows. Forgive all our sins and transgressions; draw us closer to the cross that we may be drawn closer to thee and to one another. Bless us that we may be better prepared to walk in the newness of life. And we shall praise thee together with the Father and the Holy Spirit, world without end. Amen. (102)

223 The Seven Last Words (Luke 23:32-43; John 19:25-27; Luke
        23:43; Matthew 27:46; John 19:28-30a; Luke 23:46)
Two others also, who were criminals, were led away to be put to death with him. And when they came to the place which is called The Skull, there they crucified him, and the criminals, one on the right and one on the left. And Jesus said, "Father, forgive them; for they know not what they do." And they cast lots to divide his garments. And the people stood by, watching; but the rulers scoffed at him, saying, "He saved others; let him save himself, if he is the Christ of God, his Chosen One!" The soldiers also mocked him, coming up and offering him vinegar, and saying, "If you are the King

of the Jews, save yourself!" There was also an inscription over him, "This is the King of the Jews."

One of the criminals who were hanged railed at him, saying, "Are you not the Christ? Save yourself and us!" But the other rebuked him, saying, "Do you not fear God, since you are under the same sentence of condemnation? And we indeed justly; for we are receiving the due reward of our deeds; but this man has done nothing wrong." And he said, "Jesus, remember me when you come in your kingly power." And he said to him, "Truly, I say to you, today you will be with me in Paradise."

Standing by the cross of Jesus were his mother, and his mother's sister, Mary the wife of Clopas, and Mary Magdalene. When Jesus saw his mother, and the disciple whom he loved standing near, he said to his mother, "Woman, behold your son!" Then he said to the disciple, "Behold your mother!" And from that hour the disciple took her to his own home.

It was now about the sixth hour, and there was darkness over the whole land until the ninth hour.

And about the ninth hour Jesus cried with a loud voice, "Eli, Eli, lama sabach-tha-ni?" that is, "My God, my God, why hast thou forsaken me?"

After this Jesus, knowing that all was now finished, said (to fulfill the scripture), "I thirst." A bowl full of sour wine stood there; so they put a sponge full of the wine on hyssop and held it to his mouth. When Jesus had received the wine, he said, "It is finished."

Then Jesus, crying with a loud voice, said, "Father, into thy hands I commit my spirit!" And having said this he breathed his last.

Hymns for the Lenten Season: "Again, O Lord and Savior" "Ah, Dearest Jesus" "Alas! And Did My Savior Bleed" "Behold the Lamb of God" "Beneath the Cross of Jesus" "Cross of Jesus, Cross of Sorrow" "Forty Days and Forty Nights" "Go to Dark Gethsemane" "In the Cross of Christ I Glory" "In the Hour of Trial" "It Is Finished!" "Jesus, Refuge of the Weary" "King of My Soul, a Crown of Thorns" "Lord, When Thy Kingdom Comes, Remember Me" "Lord, Who Throughout These Forty

Days" "Man of Sorrows, Now My Soul Shall Greet Thee" "My Faith Looks Up to Thee" "Near the Cross Her Vigil Keeping" "Now All Is Still" "O Come and Mourn with Me Awhile" "O Jesus, We Adore Thee" "O Lamb of God, Still Keep Me" "O Sacred Head, Now Wounded" "Our Sins, Our Sorrows" "There Is a Green Hill Far Away" " 'Tis Midnight; and on Olive's Brow" "When I Survey the Wondrous Cross"

224 **Offertory Sentence and Prayer** (Matthew 16:24b)
If any man would come after me, let him deny himself and take up his cross and follow me.

O God, who lovest those who hear thy word and keep it in faithful hearts, be pleased to bless this offering for the spreading of thy saving message among thy people. Grant that an ever-increasing number may hear thy word and keep it. We pray in the name of him who sustains us all. Amen.

(103)

✳

Eastertide

EASTER DEVOTIONS

Prelude

Hymn: "Christ the Lord Is Risen Today" or "Jesus Christ Is Risen Today"

225 **Opening Sentences** (*to be read responsively*)
I am the resurrection and the life; he who believes in me, though he die, yet shall he live, and whoever lives and believes in me shall never die.

He is risen.
The Lord is risen indeed.

ALL: *Thanks be to God, who gives us the victory through our Lord Jesus Christ.*

The Doxology *(to be sung by all)*

226   A Confession of Sins

O almighty God, who didst bring from the dead our Lord Jesus, we acknowledge that we are unworthy of thy redeeming grace. We have not believed thy promises, nor have we known the things that belong to our peace. Our hearts have not burned within us as we have heard his Word. We have not trusted in his redeeming power, and have not overcome evil with good. But now in penitence we come to thee, beseeching thy forgiveness. Mercifully pardon us, and restore unto us the joy of thy salvation; for Jesus Christ's sake.   Amen.   (127 ad)

Scripture Lesson: Matthew 28:1-10 or John 20:1-10

Apostles' Creed *(in unison)*

Hymn: "The Day of Resurrection" or "Jesus Lives and So Shall I"

227   An Easter Prayer

Praise be to thee, O Father, who didst raise up thy Son from the dead and give him glory, that our faith and hope might be in thee. Praise be to thee, O Lord Almighty, Jesus Christ, the resurrection and the life, who as on this day by thy glorious resurrection didst bring life and immortality to light. Praise be to thee, O Holy Spirit, who dost send abroad the love of Christ in our hearts, and makest us to rejoice in the hope of glory. All praise and thanks, dominion and power be unto thee, O holy and blessed Trinity, now and forevermore.   (15)

O heavenly Father, we commend to thy merciful care all who are in any way afflicted. Relieve those who suffer; restore health and strength, as thou dost will, to those who are sick. In Christ, who is the resurrection and the life, let the heavy-laden find strength to endure and those who are in the valley of the shadow see the light of life eternal. Give to those in sorrow or loneliness the assurance that nothing can ever separate them from thy love, which is in Christ Jesus our Lord. (127)

Gracious Lord, we remember that thou didst accompany thy two disciples as they journeyed to Emmaus. We, too, have a journey; we have a pilgrimage to perform. Our Emmaus is a distant though happy land. Do thou go with us, O Lord: Be our companion; guide us, uphold us, strengthen us, make our hearts to burn within us, and evermore manifest thyself to our souls in gracious and in heavenly power; for thine own name's sake we ask it. Amen. (35)

Hymn: "The Strife Is O'er" or "Alleluia! Alleluia! Hearts to Heaven"

228 Benediction (Hebrews 13:20-21)

Now may the God of peace who brought again from the dead our Lord Jesus, the great shepherd of the sheep, by the blood of the eternal covenant, equip you with everything good that you may do his will, working in you that which is pleasing in his sight, through Jesus Christ; to whom be glory for ever and ever. Amen.

ADDITIONAL WORSHIP AIDS

229 An Easter Invocation

O merciful and all-powerful God, who didst raise Jesus Christ from the dead, we invoke thy presence and inspiration, beseeching thee to renew our inner life that we may seek those things which are above. Send ministering spirits to roll away the stones from our hearts, that we may believe, even if we have not seen; that we may walk by faith as well as by sight; that we may trust and not be afraid. Then equip us with everything good, working in us that which is pleasing in thy sight. We pray through Jesus Christ, to whom with thee and the Holy Spirit be glory for ever and ever. Amen. (102)

230 The Gate of Everlasting Life

Almighty God, who through thy Son Jesus, our Lord, hast opened to us the gate of everlasting life, we humbly beseech thee that being raised out of the death of sin into the life of faith and holiness, we may live henceforth wholly unto thee, and may continue in such innocency and godliness that death may be robbed of its sting and the grave of its victory. We pray through the same Jesus, who was dead and liveth forever.   Amen.   (22)

Ascensiontide and Pentecost

WORSHIP AIDS FOR ASCENSIONTIDE

Ascension Day is forty days after Easter. The Sunday following is the sixth Sunday after Easter.

Scripture: Luke 24:49-53 or Acts 1:1-11 or Mark 16:14-20

Hymns: "Crown Him with Many Crowns" and "All Hail the Power of Jesus' Name"

231   Prayer for Ascension Day
O Lord Jesus Christ, who on this day didst ascend into the heavens, grant that we may rise with thee above all wicked thoughts and evil desires. Lift up our hearts to the throne of thy holiness, and make us dwell with thee, now and hereafter. We pray through thee, who livest and reignest, with the Father and the Holy Spirit, one God, world without end.   Amen.   (132)

PENTECOST (WHITSUNDAY) DEVOTIONS

Pentecost is seven weeks after Easter, occurring between May 10 and June 13.

Prelude

Hymn: "O Spirit of the Living God" or "Spirit of God, Descend upon My Heart"

232   Opening Sentences (Psalm 139:7-10; *to be read responsively*)

Whither shall I go from thy Spirit?
Or whither shall I flee from thy presence?
If I ascend to heaven, thou art there!
If I make my bed in Sheol, thou art there!
If I take the wings of the morning
And dwell in the uttermost parts of the sea,
Even there thy hand shall lead me,
And thy right hand shall hold me.

Doxology

Scripture Reading: Acts 2:1-11 or Isaiah 61; or the following verses on symbols and emblems of the Holy Spirit:

Dove—Matthew 3:16: And when Jesus was baptized, he went up immediately from the water, and behold, the heavens were opened and he saw the Spirit of God descending like a dove and alighting on him.

Fire—Matthew 3:11: I baptize you with water for repentance, but he who is coming after me is mightier than I, whose sandals I am not worthy to carry; he will baptize you with the Holy Spirit and with fire.

Rain—Ezekiel 34:26: And I will make them and the places round about my hill a blessing; and I will send down the showers in their season; they shall be showers of blessing.

Tongues—Acts 2:3-4: And there appeared to them tongues as of fire, distributed and resting on each one of them. And they were all filled with the Holy Spirit and began to speak in other tongues, as the Spirit gave them utterance.

Voice—Isaiah 6:8: And I heard the voice of the Lord saying, "Whom shall I send, and who will go for us?" Then said I, "Here I am! Send me."

Hymn: "Holy Spirit, Truth Divine" or "Breathe on Me, Breath of God"

233   Prayer for Enlightenment and Guidance *(by the leader)*
Most merciful and gracious God, Father of our Lord Jesus Christ, and through him our Father and the source of all our mercies, lift upon us, we beseech thee, the light of thy countenance, and grant unto us thy favor which is life, and thy loving-kindness which is better than life. Give us thankful hearts for all thy benefits bestowed upon us from day to day, and help us to show forth our gratitude, not only with our lips but in our lives, by striving in all our labors to glorify thy holy name. Strengthen us for the faithful discharge of our duties during the week upon which we have now entered. May we constantly look unto him who is the author and finisher of our faith, who suffered and died, and rose again, that we might die unto sin and live unto holiness. Enlighten and guide us by thy Holy Spirit; prepare us for our several callings during this present life and for the peace and joy of the life to come; and unto thy name, Father, Son, and Holy Spirit, be all honor and glory, world without end.   Amen.   (15)

The Lord's Prayer *(in unison)*

Hymn: "Blest Be the Tie That Binds" *(one or more stanzas)*

234   Benediction
Grace, mercy, and peace from God the Father, Son, and Holy Spirit be with you henceforth and forever.   Amen.   (127)

ADDITIONAL WORSHIP AIDS

235   An Invocation
O God our Father, who hast promised thy Holy Spirit to all who earnestly desire this heavenly gift, we beseech thee, prepare our hearts to receive him, that being guided by his light, we may see the path that leads to thee, and being filled with his power, may walk therein. Forgive us our sins, and establish us in purity, to the glory of thy holy name. Through Jesus Christ our Lord, we pray.   Amen.
                                                               (145)

236 With Christians of Every Race and Nation

O God of the universe, who art nigh unto all who call upon thee in spirit and truth, through thy Holy Spirit inspire and strengthen us who are assembled in this fellowship of prayer, that with Christians of every race and nation we may praise thy power. We pray for the sake of Jesus Christ our Lord. Amen. (103)

237 Remember Thy Whole Church

O Lord of heaven and earth, who hast promised to reveal thy glory by Jesus Christ among all the nations, remember, we beseech thee, thy holy church throughout all the world. Unite all who profess and call themselves Christians in the bond of a living faith as the body of Christ, and so replenish them and us with the grace of thy Holy Spirit that we may bring forth abundantly the fruits of peace and good works, and may turn many to righteousness through the preaching of the gospel. And grant that, having persevered in the way of godliness to the end, we may with prophets, apostles, martyrs, confessors, and saints of all ages, come into full communion with thee, and with one another, in thine eternal and glorious kingdom. We pray through our Lord and Savior Jesus Christ. Amen. (130)

6

Devotional Aids for Special Days

❋

Universal Bible Sunday

UNIVERSAL BIBLE SUNDAY is usually observed on the second Sunday in December.

Prelude

Hymn: "O Word of God Incarnate" or "Holy Lord, Holy Lord"

238   **Opening Sentences** (Jeremiah 9:23-24; *to be read responsively*)
   Thus says the Lord: "Let not the wise man glory in his wisdom, let not the mighty man glory in his might, let not the rich man glory in his riches.

   But let him who glories glory in this, that he understands and knows me, that I am the Lord who practice steadfast love, justice, and righteousness in the earth; for in these things I delight," says the Lord.

The Doxology

239   **Call to Confession** (1 John 1:8-9; *to be read responsively*)
If we say we have no sin, we deceive ourselves, and the truth is not in us.

   If we confess our sins, he is faithful and just, and will forgive our sins and cleanse us from all unrighteousness.

240   Confession of Sins

Almighty God, who hast revealed thyself in a sacred book, we confess unto thee that we have not read its teachings, pondered its precepts, nor even opened its pages as often as we should have. Have mercy upon us, and incline our hearts toward thee, whose ways are higher than our ways, and whose thoughts are higher than our thoughts. Through Jesus Christ our Lord, we pray.   Amen.   (102)

Scripture Lesson: Luke 8:11-15 or John 5:39-47

Leader: Thy Word is a lamp to my feet and a light to my path.

An Affirmation of Faith (such as Psalm 23)

241   A Litany or Responsive Prayer

Almighty and gracious God, for showing us what thou art like and telling us what we should become,
   We thank thee.
For inspiring patriarchs and prophets, saints and martyrs,
   We thank thee, O God.
Most especially for revealing thyself to us in Jesus Christ,
   Do we thank thee, our Father.
We praise thee for thy Word which is a lamp to our feet and a light to our path.
   Grant us grace and peace through knowledge of thee and thy son Jesus Christ.
Through thy Word bestow help and light day by day.
   And make us firm in the faith of our fathers;
   That the kingdoms of the world might be transformed into the kingdom of thy Son, even Jesus Christ our Lord.   Amen.   (102)

Hymn: "Holy Bible, Book Divine" or "Break Thou the Bread of Life"

The Lord's Prayer *(in unison)*

Postlude

ADDITIONAL WORSHIP AIDS

242   For a Quickening of Faith

O Father and God of all comfort, grant us through thy Word and Holy Spirit a firm, happy, and grateful faith whereby we may readily overcome this and every other trial, and at length realize that it is the truth when thy dear Son himself says: "Be of good cheer, I have overcome the world."   Amen.   (70)

243   For Grace to Retain God's Word

O merciful God, who art always ready to reveal thyself to the children of men, give us eyes to see, ears to hear, and hearts to understand thy Word. And help us so to retain thy truth that we may obey thy law all the days of our life. Through Jesus Christ our Lord, we pray.   Amen.   (102)

244   For Patience and Comfort of God's Word

Blessed Lord, who hast caused all Holy Scriptures to be written for our learning, grant that we may in such wise hear them, read, mark, learn, and inwardly digest them, that by patience and comfort of thy holy Word we may embrace, and ever hold fast, the blessed hope of everlasting life, which thou hast given us in our Savior Jesus Christ.   Amen.   (126)

New Year's Eve

THE DEVOTIONS that follow are for use on an evening near New Year's Day. Worship services can be enhanced by making a copy of the program available to each member present.

Prelude

245   Call to Worship (Psalm 34:1-3; *to be read responsively*)
> I will bless the Lord at all times;
> *His praise shall continually be in my mouth.*
> My soul makes its boast in the Lord;
> Let the afflicted hear and be glad.
> *O magnify the Lord with me,*
> *And let us exalt his name together!*

The Doxology

246   Invocation
Everlasting God, who in thy providence hast blessed us in the year now drawing to a close, watch over us in thy mercy, especially in our worship now, that our hearts may be directed to thee, who art the source and end of all our days. Through Jesus Christ our Lord, we pray.   Amen.   (102)

Hymn: "Another Year Is Dawning" or "For Thy Mercy and Thy Grace" or "O Worship the King" or "Joyful, Joyful, We Adore Thee"

Old Testament Lesson: Psalm 90 (*This may be read responsively; it is found among the responsive readings of many hymnals.*)

Gloria Patri

247   Prayer of Confession
Almighty and most merciful God, we acknowledge and confess that we have sinned against thee in thought, word, and deed; that we have not loved thee with all our heart and soul, with all our mind and strength; and that we have not loved our neighbor as ourselves. We beseech thee, O God, to forgive what we have been, to help us to amend what we are, and of thy mercy to direct what we shall be; so that we may henceforth walk in the way of thy commandments, and do those things which are pleasing in thy sight. Through Jesus Christ our Lord, we pray.   Amen.   (127)

New Testament Lesson: Matthew 6:19-34 or Philippians 3:7-14

248   Prayer of Thanksgiving
Glory be to thee, O God, for all thy goodness to us and to all men:
For the world in which thou hast placed us, with all its wonder and
beauty; for life and health, for food and clothing; for friends and
homes; for thy care that guards us always, and thy faithfulness that
never fails; most of all for Jesus Christ, thine only Son, our Savior,
who came into this world and died for us upon the cross and who
hath revealed to us the love that passeth knowledge. For all these
things we praise thee, O God, Father, Son, and Holy Spirit, world
without end.   Amen.   (127)

Response: Dresden Amen or Threefold Amen or "Hear Our Prayer,
    O Lord"

Hymn: "Standing at the Portal" or "Our God, Our Help in Ages
    Past"

249   Prayer of Supplication
Search us, O God, and try our hearts; prove us and know our
thoughts, and see if there be any wickedness in us, and lead us in
the way everlasting. We know not what a day may bring forth, but
thou art the same yesterday, today, and forever. O thou who art the
everlasting refuge of the sons of men, in thee do we put our trust.
Hear us and help us, we beseech thee, for the sake of Jesus Christ
our Lord.   Amen.   (35)

Hymn: "Ring Out, Wild Bells, to the Wild Sky"

250   Benediction (Numbers 6:24-26 ad)
    The Lord bless us and keep us:
    The Lord make his face to shine upon us, and be gracious to us:
    (All) The Lord lift up his countenance upon us, and give us peace.
Amen.

(The church bells may be rung or the chimes played on the organ
as New Year greetings are exchanged.)

ADDITIONAL WORSHIP AIDS

251 A New Year's Prayer
Ever-living God, by whose mercy we have come to the gateway of
another year, grant that we may enter it with humble and grateful
hearts; and confirm our resolution, we beseech thee, to walk more
closely in thy way; and labor more faithfully in thy service, according to the teaching and example of thy Son our Lord. Let not the
errors and offenses of the past cling to us, but pardon us and set us
free, that with a purer purpose and a better hope, we may renew our
vows of thy presence, and set forth under the guidance of thy Spirit,
to travel in that path which shineth more and more unto the perfect
day of thy heavenly kingdom.   Amen.   (14)

252 A Prayer for the New Year
Our Father, since we have never gone this way before we would ask
thee at the very beginning of the New Year to take our hand in thine
and lead us step by step and day by day until our sojourn here is
ended and we see thee face to face in the land that is fairer than day.

May the coming days be filled with a high sense of the sacredness
of life and the value of time. With the dawning of each new day,
shine on us. May the numberless memories of thy patient love deliver
us from every crooked way, from every evil thought and imagination,
that when all our days on earth are done we may be set before the
presence of thy glory without blemish in exceeding joy. Through
Jesus Christ our Lord, we pray.   Amen.   (52)

Youth Sunday

YOUTH SUNDAY is usually observed on the last Sunday in January.

253 For Help to Be Friendly
Almighty and holy God, the inspirer of youth, we thank thee most
heartily for the life thou so freely givest to those who look to thee.

In the course of our lives, help us to think on the things that are worthy of praise until our minds are full of thy thoughts. Above all, grant us such sincere love for others that we may ever be friendly to all. We pray in the name of our greatest friend, Jesus Christ our Lord. Amen.   (102)

254   For Holiness

Separate us, we beseech thee, O God, from all unworthy aims and ambitions, and unite us in sympathy and helpfulness with those who seek the advancement of love of neighbors. From weakness, idleness, and insincerity, from words without thoughts and resolves without deeds, deliver us, O God; and grant that living in love and good will with all men, we may persistently follow after holiness and thy favor. Through Jesus Christ our Lord, we pray.   Amen.   (22)

255   Litany of Thanksgiving

O Lord, who hast set before us the great hope that thy kingdom shall come on earth, and hast taught us to pray for its coming, make us ever ready to thank thee for the signs of its dawning and to pray and work for the perfect day when thy will shall be done on earth as it is in heaven. For the work of thy Spirit within and beyond the bounds of thy visible church,

We thank thee, O Lord.

For the work of thy Spirit in the history of the world, through peaceful advance and through pain and tumult,

We thank thee, O Lord.

For the work of thy Spirit in the history of our own country, through its heroes and leaders, in statecraft, law, and industry,

We thank thee, O Lord.

For the work of thy Spirit in science and commerce, in literature and art,

We thank thee, O Lord.

For the work of thy Spirit in the slow triumph of truth over error,

We thank thee, O Lord.

For the work of thy Spirit in the growing desire for true brother-hood, between men of every class and nation,
We thank thee, O Lord.

For the work of thy Spirit in the spread of education and in the development of a fuller life for individuals with healthier surroundings and better conditions,
We thank thee, O Lord.

For the work of thy Spirit in the deepening sense of human worth in all nations and classes and in the growing reverence for womanhood and childhood,
We thank thee, O Lord.

For the work of thy Spirit in the church, which will not cease until it joins all nations and kindred and tongues and peoples into one great family, to thy praise and glory,
We thank thee, O Lord. Amen. (129)

256 A Prayer for Youth

Dear Christ, thou hast ever been the one to whom thoughtful youth have pledged their strength of body, their nimbleness of mind, and their portion of talent and of skill. For thou alone dost call us to that in life which is most worth living for. Be not far from the hearts that need thee. Be not hidden from minds that trust thee. Be not distant from those who depend upon thy encouragement, counsel, and guidance. In the days of our youth, we seek, O Christ, thy influence to shape our lives for noble purposes and to mold our minds to thy will and to fashion our bodies as living altars. We praise and bless thee, O Christ, for the strength and endurance of youth, for the companionship of neighborhood chums and school friends, for the training of our minds by loving parents and self-sacrificing teachers, and for the bright prospects that lie ahead. May we be worthy of those who love us. May we be honest toward those who trust us. May we be loyal toward those who need us. And may we, most of all, be worthy children of thy kingdom, for we know, O Christ, that thou dost call us, even in our youth, to be thy disciples. When temptations sneer and evil tantalizes, give us courage not only to resist but to be-

come disciples who will challenge and encourage those with whom
we work and play.   Amen.   (139)

257   For a Youth Conference (*to be read responsively*)
To assist in keeping our young people in the fellowship of thy
church,
We need thy help, O Lord.
To promote growth among all youth in understanding and serv-
ing thy Word,
We need thy help, O Lord.
To assist one another in preparation for a life of service to thee
and mankind,
We need thy help, O Lord.
To develop an active love for the announcement of forgiveness
through Christ to all near at hand and afar off,
We need thy help, O Lord.
To foster godliness and true enjoyment in our social life and
recreation,
We need thy help, O Lord.
To encourage gifts and acts of service to all less fortunate than
ourselves,
We need thy help, O Lord.
To build close ties and deep loyalties to our Christian homes,
We need thy help, O Lord.
To guide one another through organized youth activities in our
congregations,
We need thy help, O Lord.
To unite all youth who love thee, the only true God, and Jesus
Christ whom thou hast sent,
We need thy help, O Lord.   (91)

Scripture Lessons: Philippians 3:13-16; Matthew 21:28-32; Psalm
    119:17-32; Psalm 104:1-23; Proverbs 8:10-21; Proverbs 17:3-17

Hymns: "Now in the Days of Youth"   "Purer Yet and Purer"
"Shepherd of Eager Youth"

Brotherhood Day or Race Relations Sunday

THOUGH these devotions may be used more frequently on Race Relations Sunday, near Lincoln's birthday, or in connection with other brotherhood observances during February, they are appropriate for any time during the year. Two or three people may share in conducting a program based on the following devotional aids.

Prelude

258 Invocation
"Lord God of Hosts, be with us yet, lest we forget—lest we forget!" Cause us to remember thy goodness in ages past, and to rely on thy promises for tomorrow. For today may we do justly, love mercy, and walk humbly with thee. Weld us together as a people and to thee as our God. Bring thy healing presence to bear on our broken fellowship and through this worship guide us into mutual concern and Christian brotherhood. This we ask in the name of him who went about doing good, even Jesus Christ our Lord. Amen. (118)

Hymn: "Where Cross the Crowded Ways of Life" or "In Christ There Is No East or West"

Scripture Lesson: Romans 12:3-17 or 1 Corinthians 12:12-26

The Lord's Prayer

ADDITIONAL WORSHIP AIDS

259 Free Us from Prejudice
O God, our Father, in whose eyes all men are equally precious, regard with favor, we beseech thee, this assembly of thy children. Move among us mightily with thy loving spirit. Free us altogether from every prejudice and hatred so that we and the church we represent may be light in the darkness of our time. And unto thee, author of peace and concord among men and nations, be the praise and the glory. Amen. (141)

260   For the Sensitivity of Brothers

O thou Father of all children of men, create within our hearts the sense of brotherhood. May no act of ours be merely a gesture of friendship but a sincere expression of our feeling that we are altogether, whether red, yellow, black, or white, children of thy creation, made in thy image. May our love for our fellows know no boundaries; may it draw no color line; may it take no account of nationality. We are all thine. May we all belong to each other. We pray in the name of our Elder Brother, Jesus.   Amen.   (87)

261   A Litany of Unity

O God, who hast created us in thine own image and who bestowest upon every man in the world the dignity of divine sonship,

Receive our common offering of thanksgiving and praise.

O Lover and Savior of mankind, who yearnest to reconcile all men to thyself and to break down between them every wall of hatred and segregation,

Receive our common offering of thanksgiving and praise.

O Holy Spirit, who dwellest in the hearts of the people of every race and kindred and tongue,

Hear in mercy the prayers of the multitude of thy children.

For our easy forgetting of thee, for the haughty pride we have in our small might, and for the terrible blindness which shuts out thy glory from human life,

Hear in mercy the prayers of thy people.

Save us, O God, from the sins that cruelly divide us, setting us at one another's throats as if we were beasts and not the children of the Most High;

Save us, O God, from our sins of division and strife.

Create in us a clean heart, renew in us a right spirit, and lead us out of this evil wilderness into the good homeland of brotherhood and righteousness and peace;

Redeem us, O God, from our wanderings and bring us home.

Give unto us beauty for ashes, the oil of gladness for mourning, and the garment of praise for the spirit of heaviness;

Restore unto us, we beseech thee, the joy of thy salvation.

Blessed be the Lord God, the God of Israel, who only doeth wondrous things, and blessed be his glorious name forever;

And let the whole earth be filled with his glory. Amen. (141)

Scripture Lessons: 1 Thessalonians 4:9-12; Mark 3:31-35; Isaiah 56: 1-8; Psalm 49:5-15; Proverbs 25:14-28

Hymns: " 'Thy Kingdom Come,' on Bended Knee" "Lift Up Your Heads, Ye Gates of Brass" "Hail to the Lord's Anointed" "Eternal God, Whose Power Upholds" "O God of Truth, Whose Living Word" "At Length There Dawns the Glorious Day"

❋

A Patriotic Day

THE DEVOTIONS that follow are for use on such special days as Flag Day, Independence Day, or the birthdays of national patriots.

262   For Our Freedom

We thank thee, Father, for the freedom and opportunities we have in our land. It is all from thee, for thou hast blessed us far above what we deserve. Keep us, as a people, in thy fear, and grant to us and those who rule over us thy guidance and protection; for Jesus' sake. Amen. (88)

263   For a Righteous America

We pray, O Lord, that the flag of this nation may ever be an emblem of liberty, justice, and truth. May its white speak to us of purity, its red of courage, and its blue of the eternal home beyond the stars. Bless America. Mercifully protect us, O God, from civil strife and the jealousies of race and class. Purge the land from its evils, and fill it with the spirit of Christ. Grant peace, prosperity, and happiness to us all, and above all grant that our land may become more and more a righteous nation. For Jesus' sake, we pray. Amen. (30 ad)

264   For a Righteous Canada

O Lord our heavenly Father, King of kings, and Lord of lords, bestow thy favor upon our most gracious sovereign Queen Elizabeth, and give her the grace of thy Holy Spirit, that she may do thy will and walk in thy way; give wisdom to those who sit in parliament and the legislature; and so govern the affairs of this land that we may live in righteousness and prosperity; through Jesus Christ our Lord.   Amen.   (16)

265   For Our Country and God's Glory

Almighty God, give us, we pray, the power to discern clearly right from wrong and allow all our works and actions to be governed thereby and by the laws of this land, so that all may work for the good of our beloved country and for thy glory.   Amen.   (29)

266   For Our Country

God of our fathers, who hast blessed us with the joy of living in a land of freedom and hast given to us so many rich ways of serving thy people, in our homes, in the centers of trade, and in the churches and schools and industries of our land, hear our prayer for our country today. Let it continue to be a land in which thy children shall know no lord and master but thee, and no fear but the fear of God. Let thy love find its way into mankind's heart the whole world over, that the Prince of Peace may have his way in his world, now, and in all the years to be; for his dear name's sake.   Amen.   (34)

Salute to the American Flag

I pledge allegiance to the flag of the United States of America and to the republic for which it stands: one nation under God, indivisible, with liberty and justice for all.

Hymn Response to the American Flag: "My Country, 'Tis of Thee" or "O Beautiful for Spacious Skies"

Salute to the Christian Flag

I pledge allegiance to the Christian flag and to the Savior for whose kingdom it stands: one brotherhood, uniting all mankind in service and love.

Hymn Response to the Christian Flag: "Fling Out the Banner"

Scripture Lessons: 1 Peter 2:9-10; Psalm 33; Deuteronomy 10:12-15; 11:1-9; Joshua 1:1-9; Hebrews 11:1-26

Other Hymns: "God Bless our Native Land" "God of Our Fathers Whose Almighty Hand" "Not Alone for Mighty Empire" "Faith of Our Fathers" "God of Grace and God of Glory"

Rural Life Sunday

RURAL LIFE SUNDAY is observed on the fifth Sunday after Easter.

267 Call to Worship (Psalm 24:1-5; *to be read responsively*)
The earth is the Lord's and the fullness thereof, the world and those who dwell therein;
For he has founded it upon the seas,
And established it upon the rivers.
Who shall ascend the hill of the Lord?
And who shall stand in his holy place?
He who has clean hands and a pure heart,
Who does not lift up his soul to what is false, and does not swear deceitfully.
(All) He will receive blessing from the Lord,
And vindication from the God of his salvation.

268 Opening Sentence and Invocation (Psalm 24:1-2)
The earth is the Lord's and the fullness thereof, the world and those who dwell therein; for he has founded it upon the seas, and established it upon the rivers.
We humbly acknowledge, O God, that our towering cities, our mighty industrial plants, our institutions of science and learning, our wealth and prosperity depend upon and draw life from the good earth with all its latent and life-giving powers.

Accept our worship and praise, O God, for the riches of our countryside, and we entreat thee to keep us ever mindful of our dependence upon thee for this source of our prosperity, power, and prestige. Enable us to conserve nature's resources, develop them wisely, and use them faithfully so that we may not be prodigal wasters but good stewards of thine abundant mercies. To this end, through our worship, enlighten our minds, control our emotions, and empower our hands and feet.

In Christ's blessed name, we pray.   Amen.   (62)

269   **The Divine Landscaper** *(to be read responsively)*
Our Father, who didst create the earth in infinite variety,
We praise thee.
As the Maker of all, the divine Landscaper and great Designer,
We praise thee.
As thou didst use fertile valleys, river bottoms, plains in undulating grandeur, plateaus, gentle hills, and lofty mountains in thy divine architecture,
We praise thee.
As thou didst form the oceans and the seas, and set the rivers and lakes like gems in the landscape,
We praise thee.
As thou didst so beautifully clothe the world with trees, shrubs and grass,
We praise thee.
We admire thy works and glory in them, O thou divine Creator. Enable us to search thee out until thou, who didst landscape the earth, dost also fashion our souls.
Amen.   (109)

270   **In Gratitude**
Almighty Creator, whose hand has touched all the glorious world about us, we pause on this Rural Life Sunday in deep gratitude for the bounties of thy love so graciously bestowed upon us. Because we

do not deserve the many wonders at our fingertips, we are made more aware of thy inestimable and never-failing love. Accept our sincere thanks, and show us through thy holy Word how to use these many gifts to glorify thy holy name. Amen. (144)

271 Prayer for Stewardship of the Soil

Our God and Creator, we bring thee our praise for the beauty of thy creation. In love for thy children, thou hast prepared our wonderful habitation. Give us wisdom so that we might be good stewards of the soil and the streams and the forests. In wisdom hast thou set them upon the earth. May we not destroy them through any selfishness or folly. We ask thy blessing upon thy creation so that the fields and orchards and gardens might bring forth abundance. Let thy sunshine and rain come upon the earth so that the beasts of the field and the growing plants might be made ready for the needs of men.

In all their labors give gladness to those who prepare the soil and care for the growing fruits and crops. As they gather the product of their toil and thy blessing, may they reap with rejoicing. Confer thy favor upon all migrant workers so that they may gain greater justice and fellowship with their fellow men and a keen sense of fellow-laboring with thee. Give us all a spirit of thankfulness so that men everywhere might learn to share the abundance of the Lord. In our Savior's name, we pray. Amen. (117)

272 To the Ruler of All the Earth

Our Father in heaven, Lord of field and forest, hill and stream, we thank thee for the manifestation of thy power in all growing things. Fruitful soil, quickening sunlight, and favorable rains are thy good gifts to us. As thou hast made us to have dominion over all the work of thy hands, help us, by thy Spirit, to enter into our heritage, esteeming it a high calling to be thy husbandmen. Help us to be mindful of thy partnership in all the cultivation of our gardens and the care of our flocks and herds. And when the ground hath wrought forth plentifully and earth hath yielded her increase, may we know that thou hast given us our daily bread, and may we give thee thanks in Jesus' name.   Amen.   (51)

Scripture Selections: Luke 8:5-15; Genesis 41:39-57; Matthew 25: 14-30

Hymns: "This Is My Father's World"   "O God Who Workest Hitherto"   "For the Beauty of the Earth"   "I Sing the Mighty Power of God"   "Joyful, Joyful, We Adore Thee"   "I Thank Thee, Lord, for Strength of Arm"   "Now Thank We All Our God" "Fairest Lord Jesus"

Festival of the Christian Home (Mother's Day)[1]

273   For All Mothers

O God, we offer thee praise and benediction for the ministries of motherhood in human life. We bless thee for our own dear mothers who built up our lives by theirs; who bore us in travail and loved us the more for the pain we gave; who nourished us at their breasts and hushed us to sleep in the warm security of their arms. We thank thee for their tireless love, for their voiceless prayers, for the agony with which they followed us through our sins and won us back, for the Christly power of sacrifice and redemption in mother love. We pray thee to forgive us if in thoughtless selfishness we have taken their love as our due without giving the tenderness which they craved as their sole reward. And if the great treasure of a mother's life is still spared to us, may we do for her feebleness what she did for ours.   Amen.   (99)

274   For Mother and the Home

O God of compassion, accept, in thy endless mercy, the thanksgiving of our hearts for our mothers, and all they have meant to us. We

_____

[1] Worship aids given in the following section on Christian Family Week are also applicable to this theme.

thank thee for every ideal held, for every step taken, but most of all for the ardent love in their hearts. Create in us now such devotion and love for thee that we too may help to build Christlike homes. Through Jesus Christ our Lord, we pray. Amen. (102)

275 For the Whole Family of Man

O God of love, who hast gathered the children of men into families and didst bless especially the mother and home of our Lord Jesus, bless the mothers and homes of our present day that through the worship of thy name the whole family of man may receive thy light. Through Jesus Christ our Lord, we pray. Amen. (102)

276 We Glorify Thee

Our Father, today on this festival of the Christian home, we praise and glorify thee. We give thee thanks, O God, for our Savior Jesus Christ:

For his presence as we open our homes to him,

For his strength each hour of our lives,

For his light on our daily path,

For his tender leading through our parents,

For his reproof when we sin,

For his benediction when we obey his voice,

For his life in us as we give ourselves to him,

For his transforming power to change every common task into a sacrament,

For his redeeming love which never lets us go.

O God, do thou use our homes and bless them, so that out of them may flow rivers of living water into all the thirsty earth. In Jesus' name, we pray. Amen. (107)

Scripture Lessons: Colossians 3:18-24; Ruth 1:8-11, 14-18; Titus 2: 1-10; Mark 10:2-9; 1 Samuel 1:4-20; Proverbs 31:10-31; 2 Timothy 1:1-6, 13-14

277   **God Give Us Homes** *(may be sung to tune of Yorkshire or Unde et Memores)*

God give us homes, where love and honor dwell,
Where thou art head and unseen guest, as well;
Blessing all those who live within their walls
And giving comfort when misfortune calls.
God give us homes patterned like thine above
Where we can learn of thy unselfish love.

God give us mothers who may understand
The way to lead is with a loving hand;
Asking of thee through prayer and confidence
For help in guiding those in innocence.
God give us mothers who may make a choice
'Twixt right and wrong and listen to thy voice.

God give us children eager for thy word
Round family altars where thy voice is heard,
Kneeling in prayer by flickering candle glow,
Their lives enriched, as thee they learn to know.
God bless our homes, built but of human clay;
Forgive our sins and hear a family pray.   (136)

Christian Family Week

CHRISTIAN FAMILY WEEK begins the first Sunday in May.

Prelude

Hymn: "For the Beauty of the Earth" or "O Happy Home, Where Thou Art Loved the Dearest"

278   **Opening Sentences** (Isaiah 66:1-2, 13)
Thus says the Lord:
"Heaven is my throne,
And the earth is my footstool;

What is the house which you would build for me,
And what is the place of my rest?
All these things my hand has made,
And so all these things are mine,
Says the Lord.
But this is the man to whom I will look,
He that is humble and contrite in spirit,
And trembles at my word.
As one whom his mother comforts,
So I will comfort you;
You shall be comforted in Jerusalem."

Doxology

279 A Collect

O God of love, who didst wonderfully bless the mother and home of our Lord Jesus, bless the mothers and homes of the world today, that all hearts may be willing to worship thee and obey thy commandments. Through Jesus Christ our Lord, we pray. Amen. (103)

Response: "O Thou Who Hearest Every Heartfelt Prayer" or "Hear, O Lord, Our Humble Supplication"

Scripture Reading (select one from the following)
  The Christian view of marriage: Matthew 19:3-6
  Christian nurture in the family: Deuteronomy 6:4-9
  Motives that strengthen family life: Ephesians 5:28-33
  Duties of the Christian family: Ephesians 6:1-9

A Reading (if desired)

Hymn: "Love Divine, All Loves Excelling" or "O Jesus, I Have Promised" or "I Would be True"

The Lord's Prayer

Closing Hymn: "Blest Be the Tie That Binds" (one or more stanzas)

280   Benediction

May God bless us as we seek light and strength throughout the week.
Amen.   (102)

ADDITIONAL WORSHIP AIDS

281   Beatitudes for the Home

Blessed are they who rejoice in their children;
To them is revealed the fatherhood of God.
Blessed are they who know the power of love;
They dwell in God, for God is love.
Blessed are the songful of soul;
They carry light and joy to shadowed lives.
Blessed are they that see visions;
They shall rejoice in the hidden ways of God.
Blessed are they that have understanding hearts;
To them shall be multiplied kingdoms of delight.
Blessed are the childless, loving children still;
Theirs shall be a mightier family—even as the stars of heaven.
Blessed are they whose memories we cherish;
Our thoughts add jewels to their crowns.   (93)

282   For Our Children

Our Father, we thank thee for the sacred joy and the holy mystery
of parenthood, for the love and the beauty of family life, for the
daily disciplines of selfless living, for thy gracious forgiveness of our
many failures, for constant renewal as we live in thee.

Teach us, O God, to pray for our children in accordance with thy
will. Use us to let thy divine plan unfold in them. Give us inner
eyes to see beyond this world of time into eternity, that we may want
for them not success as the world sees it, but only what thy love wills
for each one: not personal fame, but thy glory; not earthly wealth
but thy riches.

May they open the sanctuary of their hearts to thy spirit. May
they listen only to thy voice. May they carry thy radiance into the

turmoil of the world, and daily share thy energizing life with their fellow men. This we pray in Jesus' name. Amen. (107)

283   Thanks for Family Ties
O thou eternal God of all truth, who art our Father and our everlasting friend, we bring to thee the precious treasures represented in our family ties. We thank thee for the sacrifices of our fathers and mothers, our sisters and our brothers, and friends. And we know, O God, that thou art the love that unites and the love that holds together our universe. In Jesus' name, we pray. Amen. (59)

Memorial Day[1]

284   For Memorial Day
O Lord, we remember gratefully the days of old and consider the years of many generations. Brighten our hearts with the hope that once filled the lives of men who have now laid their burdens down. Deepen our dedication to those men who surrendered their youth and strength for the commonweal. May we not with fugitive minds and prodigal hands turn from the nation and church and people for which in days of peril they took up nobly and then laid down quietly the sword. But may we in quiet confidence arise from prayer to build in our lives and in the life of the state the kind of world they died to save. Give us integrity and purpose in days of struggle and give us unity of spirit and brotherhood of word and deed in the years of peace. Amen. (139)

285   Invocation
O God, who hast prepared for all who love thee, a city, having foundations, glorious beyond all human thought, receive thou the

---

[1] Memorial Sunday on page 144 offers further worship aids appropriate to this theme.

joyful songs of our pilgrimage and the praise we offer, that we may
be established in one holy fellowship with all thy saints in heaven
and on earth. Through Jesus Christ our Lord, we pray.   Amen. (145)

Scripture Lessons: John 14:1-15; Joshua 4:4-8, 21-24; Psalm 99;
    Psalm 144; Proverbs 14:26-34; Mark 12:18-27

Hymns: "Faith of Our Fathers"   "God of our Fathers, Whose Al-
    mighty Hand"   "My Country, 'Tis of Thee"   "O Beautiful for
    Spacious Skies"

Church School Day

286   Invocation

Almighty God, our heavenly Father, who has committed to thy holy
church the care and nurture of thy children, enlighten with thy wisdom those who teach and those who learn, that, rejoicing in the
knowledge of thy truth, we may worship thee and serve thee from
generation to generation. Through Jesus Christ our Lord, we pray.
Amen.   (121)

287   For Church School Day *(by the leader)*

We thank thee, our Father, for the laughter and bright smiles of
little children and for their capacity to enjoy the common things
obscured to our busy minds, for their energy of limb and their swift-
ness of thought, for their ceaseless curiosity and their simple questions, for their spontaneous good will and their ease in forgetting
unpleasantness, and for their trust and dependence on those who
show them love. Spare us from that hardness of heart which slights
their questions or rejects the generosity of their affection or turns
from their need of a helping hand or an encouraging word. Not only
because our world with its hopes and fears, its tribulations and opportunities will one day be theirs, but more because thou hast given

them in trust to our care, do we dedicate our finest hours and our deepest love to all of them. We pray in the name of him who, when others found little children to be bothersome, called them unto himself and blessed them, even Christ Jesus our Lord.   Amen. (139)

288   A Meditation-Prayer

I praise you, God, and give thanks for your great plan for growing: the helpless kitten learns to care for itself; the wee humming bird learns to fly; boys and girls learn to think, to understand, to love; each grows according to its kind.

I praise you, God, and give thanks for your great love for growing things. Please keep me growing, God, according to your plan. Amen.   (19)

289   Bless Our Children

Dear God, we thank thee and praise thee for an awakening of our conscience to our tasks as adults. Guide our minds to a full understanding and grant us the insight to see how best we can carry out thy will for each of the children brought before thee in this service. Bless them all with thy heavenly grace so that their journey through this life, in spite of sorrow and pain, may be brighter, pleasanter, because they walk with thee.

For service in thy glorious plan we dedicate ourselves and these children in the name of thy Son, Jesus Christ.   Amen.   (7)

Scripture Lessons: Psalm 8; Mark 10:13-16; 1 Samuel 3:1-18; Proverbs 23:19-26; Psalm 63:1-8; Psalm 127; Luke 18:15-27

Hymns: "We Would See Jesus" "Angel Voices, Ever Singing" "I Think When I Read That Sweet Story of Old" "Jesus, Tender Shepherd, Hear Me" "Savior, Like a Shepherd Lead Us"

❈

Father's Day

FATHER'S DAY is observed on the third Sunday in June.

290   An Invocation for Father's Day
O God, from whom every family in heaven and on earth is named,
we thank thee that thou hast revealed thyself unto us as our Father.
Each day we receive fresh tokens of thy fatherly concern for us.
Grant that we may turn to thee this day with confidence and trust
as children turn toward their father. Help us to respond to thy
love, so that we may live in harmony with all of thy children. To
that end we pray thee to bless the worship of this day, in the name
of him who taught us to say: "Our Father."   Amen.   (119)

291   Bless All Fathers
Almighty God, we thank thee that through Jesus Christ thou hast
revealed thyself as our Father in heaven. We rejoice that thou knowest our needs before we ask them. Help us all to praise thee for thy
wonderful works to the children of men. We pray that thou wouldst
bless all fathers, that they may know how to provide for their children and be good examples in Christlike living.   Amen.   (102)

292   A Prayer of Thanks for Fathers
Almighty God, our heavenly Father who makest the sun to rise on
the evil and the good and who sendest rain on the just and the un-
just, give us grace to imitate thy fatherly love for all mankind. We
offer thanks for the fathers of our community: for the part they play
in the rearing of children, for defending and providing for their
homes, and for the support they give to wider enterprises. Above all
we thank thee for their life, which enables many of us to think of
thee as our Father in heaven. Strengthen all fathers that they in
turn will help their children to be true to thee till death. In the
name of Jesus Christ our Lord, we pray.   Amen.   (102)

Scripture Lessons: Luke 15:11-32; Matthew 7:9-12; Genesis 45:9-11, 17-27; Genesis 46:29-31; Genesis 47:7-12; Deuteronomy 21:18-21; Luke 6:36-42

Hymns: "This Is My Father's World" "Faith of Our Fathers" "Rise Up, O Men of God" "God Send Us Men" "Stand Up, Stand Up for Jesus"

※

Independence Day

INDEPENDENCE DAY in the United States is celebrated by the church on July 4 or the Sunday before.

293 An Invocation

O Lord God, who art with us always to give us strength and good courage, we thank thee for our nation, for its qualities of freedom and justice, and for all other blessings. Help us to acknowledge thee as our living God and, in obedience to thy commandments, help us to become a righteous nation. We pray in the name of him who has promised freedom to all who know the truth, even Jesus Christ our Lord. Amen. (102)

294 Kindle the Pure Flame of Sacrifice

Almighty God, who on this day didst direct and inspire the hearts of our fathers to set forth the independence of these United States, we give all glory and praise to thee, the Author of our liberty, and the sure Defense of our safety. We pray that by thy grace we may be enabled to build wisely upon these foundations of freedom and of peace and that we may hold our liberties in due subjection to thy law, and in all things seek that righteousness which exalteth a nation. Kindle in our hearts the pure flame of sacrifice to our country's needs; and grant that the fires of our patriotism may shine as beacon lights upon thy holy hills, O God, and may point the ways of men toward that universal brotherhood, when the nations of the world shall be one in Jesus Christ our Lord.   Amen.   (8)

295   For Loyalty to Our Land

Almighty God, who didst bless our nation in times past, help us to be truly thankful for all thy guidance, that we may be loyal citizens of this land. Enable us to feel that thou art our God and Father, that we may be thy faithful children. Above all, inspire us in heart and soul that we may sincerely worship thee and think of the welfare of our fellow men. Through Jesus Christ our Lord, we pray.   Amen.
(102)

296   For Independence Day

Father of all men and Lord of all nations, we thank thee for oui rich heritage of freedom. We praise thee for the right to choose our work, to think and to speak our minds freely, to select those who govern us, and to worship as our consciences direct us. Help us to honor thee and those who have left us this heritage by upright and unselfish living; through Jesus Christ our Lord.   Amen.   (111)

297   God of Our Fathers

God of our fathers, and our own personal God, we thank thee for the great men of our nation who built the structure of government under which free men have lived so long.

We honor them today by our words of praise; help us to honor them by being true to the heritage they left us, and by keeping sacred the nation they made possible for us to have. Grant that the words on our coins, "In God we trust," may be a statement of truth and not a mockery. O God, live in all our institutions, in all our purposes, and in all our national leaders. In Jesus' name, we pray.   Amen.
(82)

298   For Light Along the Path

O God of our fathers, who hast blessed us with the goodly heritage of a free land and hast here made of one blood faithful men from many shores, cause the light of thy truth that our fathers followed to be no less dim along the path of their sons. In Christ's name, we pray. Amen. (139)

Labor Day Sunday

LABOR DAY SUNDAY is observed by the church on the Sunday before Labor Day.

299 For Our Daily Work

Eternal God, who hast given us to live and to labor while it is day, we give thee thanks for our daily work. For all tasks that challenge and strengthen us; for work that calls for our best; for the creative labor of the mind and the imagination; for the painstaking toil of countless patient men and women, we bless thee.

Teach us, O Lord, to see our daily duties in their timeless meaning as parts of thy purpose. Bless all who labor to earn their living and by their calling add to our common wealth. Make us mindful of those who perform inconspicuous and menial tasks no less than those whose occupations are difficult and dangerous. Rouse us to strive manfully against every condition that defrauds men and women of what they have earned, and their children of what is the right of every child. Give wisdom to employers and to leaders of labor. Strengthen and inspire the endeavors of those who work to improve the common lot. Guide those in positions of authority to devise wise laws and to administer them fairly. And lead us to build an order among men in which each will find joy in his toil and offer it as his acceptable service unto thee. We pray in the name of Christ, the master workman. Amen. (56)

300 For Labor Day Sunday

Let us not measure our daily work by the sweat of our brow only or by the monetary profit a day's toil may bring, but may we discover

in our laboring the joy of creating things worthwhile, the opportunity of cooperating with others for a noble purpose, and the satisfaction of work well done.

Turn, we pray thee, O God, all drudgery into devotion, all duty
into delight, all travail into triumph. Help us to think of work in
terms of food for children, and of toil in terms of happy homes, and
of weary and worn bodies in terms of accomplishment. May we not
waste our strength in carelessness nor our energy in shiftlessness, but
may we, as good and faithful servants, remember that thou shalt one
day call each of us to account for his stewardship. We pray in the
name of him who said, "My Father is working still, and I am working," even Jesus Christ, the carpenter of Nazareth and the builder
of thy kingdom.   Amen.   (139)

301   **Psalm of Labor** (Adapted from Proverbs 3:13-14; Ecclesiasticus
        6:18-19; 38:25-32, 34; 48:17; Wisdom of Solomon 8:72; Isaiah
        65:21, 23.)
Happy is the man who finds wisdom,
And the man who gets understanding,
For the gain from it is better than gain from silver
And its profit better than gold.
The life of him who labors and is wise,
Shall be made sweet.
If a man loves righteousness
The fruits of wisdom's labor are virtues.
How shall he become wise who holds the plow,
Who drives oxen and is occupied with their labors?
He glories in the shaft of the goad:
He will set his heart upon turning his furrows.
So is the smith sitting by the anvil,
And considering the unwrought iron:
He will set his heart upon perfecting his works,
And he will be wakeful to adorn them perfectly.
So is the potter sitting at his work,
And turning the wheel about:

He will fashion the clay with his arm,
He will apply his heart to finish the glazing.
So was he that fortified the city,
And brought water into the midst of them;
He digged the sheer rock with iron,
And builded up wells for water.
They shall not labor in vain,
For their labor is with wisdom and
    with knowledge and with skillfulness.
All these put their trust in their hands;
And each becometh wise in his own work.
Without these shall not a city be inhabited,
And men shall not sojourn nor walk up and down therein.
For these maintain the fabric of the world;
And in the handiwork of their craft is their prayer. (137)

Scripture Lessons: 1 Timothy 6:1-12; 1 Corinthians 3:6-17; Ecclesiastes 5:12, 18-20; John 8:12-20; Luke 6:43-49; Luke 12:4-9; Matthew 21:33-46

Hymns: "O Master Workman of the Race" "Jesus, Thou Divine Companion" "O Brother Man, Fold to Thy Heart Thy Brother" "Work, for the Night is Coming" "His Was No Regal Splendor"

302 An Offertory Prayer
Our Father, help us to realize anew that this offering we bring to thee truly represents our labor and hence our life. Bless not only the portion we give thee, but also the portion we keep that we might use this in accordance with thy will. We pray in the name of Jesus who gave his all for us. Amen. (72)

Christian Education Sunday

CHRISTIAN EDUCATION SUNDAY in some churches is observed in place of Rally Day or Promotion Day. It celebrates the teaching ministry of the church in the congregation, usually on a Sunday in early fall.

303   Call to Worship (Proverbs 3:13-15; 4:7b-8a; 9:10)

Happy is the man who finds wisdom,

And the man who gets understanding,

For the gain from it is better than gain from silver and its profit better than gold.

She is more precious than jewels, and nothing you desire can compare with her.

Get wisdom, and whatever you get, get insight.

Prize her highly, and she will exalt you.

The fear of the Lord is the beginning of wisdom,

And the knowledge of the Holy One is insight.

304   A Teacher's Prayer

O God, I thank thee that thou hast called me to teach thy children. Be thou the source of my strength, my understanding and patience. Bless every effort, and, dear God, may thy children under my care be drawn nearer to thy Son, Jesus Christ, that they may ever be ready to take a stand for him even if it means breaking with the crowd and standing alone for their faith.   Amen.   (61)

305   A Prayer on Christian Education Sunday (Rally Day)

Our Father, we are happy to be gathered together in thy house on this day, as we close one year of work in our church school and look forward to a new year. Forgive us if we have not taken the study of thy Word as seriously as we should have in the past. As we go into new classes and study new courses, may we be more faithful in our attendance and more conscientious in our study. Help us to grow more like Jesus, in whose name we pray.   Amen.   (101)

306   A Prayer by Erasmus

O Lord Jesus Christ, who art the way, the truth, and the life, we pray thee suffer us not to stray from thee, who art the way, nor to distrust thee, who art the truth, nor to rest in any other thing than thee, who art the life. Teach us by thy Holy Spirit what to believe, what to do, and wherein to take our rest. For thine own name's sake, we ask it. Amen.

Scripture Readings on Christian Education: Romans 15:1-6; Romans 15:1-17; 1 Corinthians 14:1-12; 1 Corinthians 14:13-33; Ephesians 5:1-20

Hymns: "Now in the Days of Youth" "Shepherd of Eager Youth" "Lord, Speak to Me That I May Speak" "Teach Me, O Lord, Thy Holy Way" "Purer Yet and Purer"

World-wide Communion Sunday

307   An Invocation
O God our heavenly Father, who for the sin of a wayward world didst send thine only Son to be our Savior and Lord, grant us now to be strengthened in that great spiritual fellowship of all who trust thee and who come unto thee through him, that with them we may be united in praising thee for thy marvelous works. We pray through the same Jesus Christ our Lord.   Amen.   (145)

308   Help Us to Be Grateful
O thou great Father of all nations and kindreds, in deep awe do we stand before thy throne on this day, remembering thy love for us, and the power of pardon thou hast bestowed upon us through our Lord. Through the elements of bread and wine, so graciously given to all who would receive, help us, O Father, to be grateful in our receiving.   Amen.   (144)

Scripture Lessons: Exodus 20:1-17; 1 John 1:5-9; Matthew 26:26-29; Luke 19:1-10; John 4:27-42; John 7:37-44; John 12:44-50

Hymns: "Jesus, Thou Joy of Loving Hearts"   "Let All Mortal Flesh

Keep Silence" "Bread of the World in Mercy Broken" "According to Thy Gracious Word" "Here, O My Lord, I See Thee Face to Face" "A Parting Hymn We Sing"

�֍

World Order Sunday

WORLD ORDER SUNDAY is usually observed on a Sunday near October 24 or November 11.

309   Call to Worship (Micah 4:2, 5)

Come, let us go up to the mountain of the Lord, to the house of the God of Jacob;
That he may teach us his ways and we may walk in his paths.
For all the peoples walk each in the name of its god,
But we will walk in the name of the Lord our God for ever and ever.

310   An Invocation

Eternal God, Creator of all mankind, prepare in the deserts of our hearts a highway for thyself. Lead us, gracious Father, in the midst of our confusion to find thy peace that passes understanding. In the power of that peace may we pray earnestly and work diligently for righteousness and harmony among the races and nations of thy world. Through Jesus Christ, the Prince of Peace, we pray.   Amen.
(116)

311   A Prayer for Those Who Take Counsel

Almighty God, from whom all thoughts of truth and peace proceed, kindle, we pray thee, in the hearts of all men the true love of peace, and guide with thy pure and peaceable wisdom those who take counsel for the nations of the earth, that in tranquillity thy kingdom may go forward, till the earth is filled with the knowledge of thy love. We ask it through Jesus Christ our Lord.   Amen.   (94)

312   A Litany of Peace

Remember, O Lord, the peoples of the world divided into many
nations and tongues. Deliver us from every evil which obstructs thy
saving purpose. From the curse of war and tyranny and all that be-
gets them,

O Lord, deliver us.

From believing and speaking lies against other nations,

O Lord, deliver us.

From narrow loyalties and selfish isolation,

O Lord, deliver us.

For having false pride in our own country,

Our Father, we ask thy forgiveness.

For failing to share with those in need in other lands,

Our Father, we ask thy forgiveness.

For putting our trust in might rather than in justice,

Our Father, we ask thy forgiveness. Through Jesus Christ our Lord,
we pray.   Amen.   (129 ad)

313   For the Coming of Christ's Kingdom

O God, who hast taught us to pray for the coming of thy kingdom
on this earth, give us grace to build our communities after the fashion
of thy kingdom, to set no boundaries about them which thou wouldst
not set, to quiet the tumult and strife within them by brotherly love,
and to work the more diligently for concord within them because
our final hope is in the city which hath foundations whose builder
and maker is God. Through Jesus Christ our Lord, we pray.   Amen.
(85)

314   Grant Success

Blessed Lord Jesus, thou Prince of peace, forgive us for our share
in the strife which disturbs our lives and the life of the world. Keep
us from the spirit of hatred and revenge, and make our hearts open
to every opportunity for bringing peace to the hearts of men. Grant
success unto every effort which is being put forth to ensure peace for
all mankind. For thy name's sake, we pray.   Amen.   (148)

315   Prayer of Confession in Time of War

Eternal Spirit of right, we come to thee with burdened hearts because of the strife which now lays waste the world. We acknowledge it to be the bitter fruit of our little wisdom and our little faith; of all that has been unrighteous in our history; of all that has made us unworthy to be called thy sons. May our spirits be cleansed to see now the right and to perform it both in war and in peace. Grant us courage to endure whatever ill may come upon us, and a steadfast purpose to fulfill the tasks which the times require.   Amen.   (137)

316   Litany in Time of National Emergency

O Lord, show thy mercy upon us.
And grant us thy salvation.
O God, make clean our hearts within us.
And take not thy Holy Spirit from us.

O thou whose might is in all moving things and in the good will of men, we give thee thanks for the unmeasured heroism of those in generations gone who have trusted in the right and offered their all in the cause of freedom.

In this our day of trial, give us equal faith and courage.

O thou light of all peoples that dwell upon the face of the earth: We remember before thee the nations that suffer the wounds and ruin of war brought upon them by the injustice and wickedness of men.

May their hearts be encouraged by the hope of earthly help and by faith in everlasting right.

We pray that thy spirit may restore wholeness of mind and heart to the many of our fellow men who have suffered the usurpation of their conscience and the misguidance of their virtue.

May every people be led to seek a peace that is just to themselves according as they desire justice for all.

Holy Spirit, in whose eternal life are held those whom we love and all the labors of our years, we commit to thee all who are called upon to do battle for the frustration of tyranny and aggression.

May they be strengthened for every task of duty and helped in every hour of darkness or of pain.

We seek the guidance of thy light for the President of our United States and for all those upon whom are laid the heavy burdens of decision for our nation.

May there be wisdom in the counsels of state and a willing spirit amongst all the people.

Light of our fathers, we give thanks for the favor of our liberties and for the assurances of future good that live in the faiths of a free church and a free state.

In all the doings of our common life and common labor, may we learn new ways of freedom and the meanings of equal regard for all.

Eternal God, enlarge our understanding and sustain our purpose until there be wrought in this present world such commerce of faiths, such customs and laws of right as shall establish peace among the nations and brighter hopes for the whole family of man. Amen.

(137)

317 For Unity Among the Nations

Dear God our heavenly Father, help us by thy grace to see the sin of war, and to strive within our own hearts and lives to promote the ways of peace. In our world of tensions and strife, bring about a unity among the nations, we pray thee, to the end that we may all live in peace, doing those things that are pleasing in thy sight. Grant unto thy people everywhere that peace of thine which passeth all understanding. Through Jesus Christ our Lord, we pray. Amen.

(148)

318 For Better Understanding

Most holy Father, we bring to thee our prayer for understanding among the peoples of the earth. Forgive us for our part in the world's hatred and strife. Purge us of pride of race and class. Wipe out our resentments of thy children in other lands. When the nations rage and imagine vain things, may we know that thou art God and that thy mercy goes out to all thy creatures. Awaken in us that spirit of

righteousness, that love and forgiveness which we have discovered in
thy Son, Jesus Christ.   Amen.   (116)

Scripture Lessons: Matthew 5:43-48; Micah 4:1-5; Isaiah 2:1-11;
    Psalm 85; 1 Samuel 15:22-31; Hosea 11:1, 3-11; Mark 12:28-37;
    Mark 9:33-37; Psalm 67; Isaiah 55:6-13

Hymns: "God of Grace and God of Glory"   "Thy Kingdom Come,
    O Lord"   "O God of Love, O King of Peace"   "In Christ There
    Is No East or West"   "These Things Shall Be: a Loftier Race"
    "Turn Back, O Man, Forswear Thy Foolish Ways"   "Eternal
    Ruler of the Ceaseless Round"   "At Length There Dawns the
    Glorious Day"   "God the Omnipotent"

Reformation Day

REFORMATION DAY is celebrated on or near October 31.

Prelude

Opening Sentences (Psalm 98:1-3; *to be read responsively*)
    O sing to the Lord a new song,
    For he has done marvelous things!
    His right hand and his holy arm have gotten him victory.
    The Lord has made known his victory,
    He has revealed his vindication in the sight of the nations.
    He has remembered his steadfast love and faithfulness to the house
of Israel.
    All the ends of the earth have seen the victory of our God.

Hymn: "Glorious Things of Thee Are Spoken" or "O Where Are
    Kings and Empires Now?"

319   Prayer of Confession
Most gracious Father in heaven, we confess our sins and shortcomings unto thee: In not loving thee with all our heart, in not obeying

thee with all our soul, in not serving thee with all our might. Have mercy upon us: Take away our guilt! And help us to love thee as we should, to obey thee as we ought, and to serve thee as we could. Through Jesus Christ our Lord, we pray. Amen. (102)

Old Testament Lesson *(may be read by the leader, or responsively if in the Psalter of your hymnal):* Psalm 46

New Testament Lesson: John 2:13-17 or Luke 12:49-53

Hymn: "The Church's One Foundation" or "Christ Is Made the Sure Foundation"

A Brief Talk *(such as the following)*

On Reformation Sunday our thoughts turn to Martin Luther, and we remember his struggle to reform and purify the church of his day, a struggle that led finally to the fullness of our Protestant Christian faith.

There is not time to speak of all Luther's achievements, but it may be helpful for us to remember that he was once a young monk, miserable and distraught because he could not be *sure* that he had earned God's love and forgiveness. He struggled to gain peace of mind, but nothing gave him peace. He could not help himself. Later, in his study of scripture, he came to realize that the forgiveness he tried so hard to earn had already been given him freely and unconditionally by God. In Christ's death upon the cross, Luther discovered the forgiveness that neither he nor any man could earn for himself.

Luther learned to give himself so fully to God that he could later advise another anxious monk: "Learn to know Christ and him crucified. Learn to praise him, and, ceasing to trust in yourself, say to him, 'Thou, Lord, art my righteousness.'" This was in the year 1516.

By 1517 Luther's thoughts were so clear and his convictions so strong that on October 31 he nailed his ninety-five theses to the door of the Wittenberg Church, indicating his willingness to defend any or all of the statements.

Four years later, when he was on trial before the emperor, he was so concerned for the victory of truth that when he was asked if he was willing to renounce his writings, he answered:

"I shall not be convinced, except by the testimony of the Scriptures, or plain reason. . . . Here I stand, I cannot do otherwise. God help me.   Amen!"

Eight years later, in a dark hour for the whole Protestant cause, he could sing:

> Let goods and kindred go,
> This mortal life also;
> The body they may kill:
> God's truth abideth still,
> His kingdom is forever.

This courageous hymn, rugged and strong in faith, became "the Battle Hymn of the Reformation," and has since been translated into 184 languages. Let us now sing this great hymn of faith, written by Martin Luther.   (102)

Hymn: "A Mighty Fortress Is Our God"

320   Prayers by Outstanding Reformers

God of all comfort, we commend to thy mercy all those upon whom any cross or tribulation is laid; the nations who are afflicted with famine, pestilence, or war; those of our brethren who suffer persecution for the sake of the gospel; all such as are in danger by sea or land; and all persons oppressed with poverty, sickness, or any infirmity of body or sorrow of mind. May it please thee to show them thy fatherly kindness in the midst of affliction, that their hearts may turn unto thee, and receive perfect consolation, healing, and deliverance from their troubles, for Christ's sake.   (21 ad)

O Thou, who art the Author of all good things in thy holy church, work mightily in all thy servants, that they may be profitable to all men, and vessels of thy mercy and grace. Control us all, and so govern our thoughts and deeds, that we may serve thee in righteousness and true holiness; and sanctify us all unto that eternal life, which we . . . wait for and expect.   (76 ab)

We thank thee, O God, the Father of our Lord Jesus Christ, that thou hast revealed thy Son to us, on whom we have believed, whom we have loved, and whom we worship. Father, into thy hands we commend our spirits. Through Jesus Christ our Lord, we pray. Amen.   (70 ab)

A Blessing
May God bless us as we seek light and strength throughout the week. Amen.   (102)

Thanksgiving

THANKSGIVING is observed on a Sunday or a weekday near Thanksgiving Day.

Prelude
Hymn: "Now Thank We All Our God" or "Come, Ye Thankful People, Come"

Opening Sentences (Psalm 92:1-2)
> It is good to give thanks to the Lord,
> *To sing praises to thy name, O Most High;*
> To declare thy steadfast love in the morning,
> *And thy faithfulness by night.*

321   Prayer of General Thanksgiving

Almighty God, Father of all mercies, we, thine unworthy servants, do give thee most humble and hearty thanks for all thy goodness and loving-kindness to us and to all men. We bless thee for our creation, preservation, and all the blessings of this life; but above all for thy boundless love in the redemption of the world by our Lord Jesus Christ; for the means of grace and the hope of glory. And we beseech thee, give us that due sense of all thy mercies, that our hearts may be sincerely thankful, and that we may show forth thy praise, not only with our lips, but in our lives; by giving up ourselves to thy service, and by walking before thee in holiness and righteousness all our days. We pray through Jesus Christ our Lord, to whom with thee and the Holy Ghost be all honor and glory, world without end.   Amen.   (125 ad)

Hymn: "Praise to God, Immortal Praise" or "O God, Beneath Thy Guiding Hand"

322   Prayer of Confession
Eternal God, in whom we live and move and have our being, whose face is hidden from us by our sins, and whose mercy we forget in the blindness of our hearts, cleanse us, we beseech thee, from all our offenses, and deliver us from proud thoughts and vain desires; that with lowliness and meekness we may draw near to thee, confessing our sins, trusting in thy grace, and finding in thee our refuge and our strength, through Jesus Christ thy Son.   Amen.   (127)

Scripture Lesson: Luke 12:13-34 or Deuteronomy 8:6-18 or Psalm 103 or Mark 11:20-26 or 1 Timothy 2:1-8

323   An Affirmation of Faith
I believe that God has made me and all creatures; that he has given me my body and soul, eyes, ears, and all my members, my reason and all my senses, also food and clothing, home and family, and all my possessions; that he daily and abundantly provides me with all the necessities of life, protects and preserves me from danger; and all this he does out of sheer fatherly and divine goodness and mercy, without any merit or worthiness on my part. For all this I am in duty bound to thank, praise, serve, and obey him. This is most certainly true.   (31 ad)

Hymn: "My God, I Thank Thee Who Hast Made" or "We Praise Thee, O God, Our Redeemer, Creator"

324 Prayer of Intercession

God of our fathers, who didst lead thine ancient people through desert wanderings into the promised land, and who didst guide our pilgrim sires across the stormy seas to lay here the foundations of this great republic, we implore thy blessing upon those who have lately come from other lands to make their home in this country. Amid strange faces and unaccustomed scenes may they feel that thou art with them. In their loneliness and homesickness may they realize that the everlasting friend is beside them, upon whom they may cast all the burden of care and anxiety. Help those about them to give them sympathy and good cheer in the spirit of Christ. May they prosper in this land of freedom and justice and opportunity, and become loyal and devoted citizens of this country of their adoption. May they be faithful followers of Christ, that they may be also fellow citizens with the saints in that liberty wherewith Christ maketh his people free.   Amen.   (12)

Hymns: "Take Thou Our Minds, Dear Lord" or "Christ of the Upward Way"

Benediction

ADDITIONAL WORSHIP AIDS

325   A Litany of Thanksgiving

For thy holy Word, in which we are shown how to live godly, sober, and useful lives, that we may glorify thee, our Father:

We praise thee and thank thee, O God.

For thy holy gospel, the story of thine infinite love for all the world, made known in the giving of Christ thy Son, who died that we might live:

We offer thee our deepest thanks, O God.

For thy church which preaches and teaches thy Word throughout the world, and whose ministry seeks to win souls for citizenship in thy kingdom of love:

We give thee our praise, O Father.

For the part we may have in the great work of preparing our com-

munity for the coming of thy kingdom, and for the chance we have
through thy church to reach out helping hands to peoples all over
the earth:

We gratefully praise thee, our Father.   Amen.   (145)

326   Thanksgiving for Our Heritage

O Lord we thank thee for the glorious heritage which thou hast
given unto us:

For the land in which we dwell;

For the freedom we have in thought, speech, and worship;

For the homes in which we dwell with the security of mutual
love and respect;

For our daily work which adds meaning to our lives as we make
ourselves useful members of thy household;

For thine abiding presence which ever renews our lives in faith,
hope, and love.

Help us ever to be aware of these manifestations of thy grace and
enable us to live day by day with a deep sense of appreciation for
thy abiding love and care; through Jesus Christ our Lord.   Amen.

(104)

Memorial Sunday

MEMORIAL SUNDAY is observed on the last Sunday of the church year.

327   A Litany (based on Psalm 145)

I will extol thee, my God and King, and bless thy name for ever
and ever. Every day I will bless thee, and praise thy name for ever
and ever.

*One generation shall laud thy works to another, and shall declare
thy mighty acts.*

Under the shadow of thy throne thy saints of every age have dwelt secure, for thou art the rock, the fortress, the defense, the sure, eternal dwelling place of all who put their trust in thee.

Our God, our help in ages past,
Thou art our hope for the years to come.

All thy works shall give thanks to thee, O Lord, and all thy saints shall bless thee. They shall speak of the glory of thy kingdom, and tell of thy power; to make known to the sons of men thy mighty acts, and the glorious splendor of thy kingdom.

Thy kingdom is an everlasting kingdom, and thy dominion endures throughout all generations. We praise thee, we bless thee, we magnify thy holy name, that thy eternal goodness extends to us and gives us a share in thy glorious kingdom.

We are unworthy of the love and mercy thou daily bestowest on us, for we are weak and sinful, and in many ways we grieve thy Holy Spirit; yet we believe thy promise to receive us and pardon us, through him who died to set us free from sin, even thy Son, our blessed Savior.

Through faith in thy abounding grace we come to thee, asking for pardon and for peace, and for strength to lead a righteous, holy life. Through Jesus Christ our Lord, we pray. Amen. (145)

328 Example of the Saints

Almighty and everlasting God, who dost enkindle the flame of love in the hearts of thy saints and dost grant to us the same faith and power of love, may we, as we rejoice in their triumphs, also follow their good example, in the spirit of Jesus Christ our Master. Amen.

(92)

Scripture Lessons: Matthew 5:1-12; 1 Corinthians 15:50-58; Luke 6:20-26; Psalm 90; John 11:11, 20-27; Revelations 14:1-3; John 5:19-29

Hymns: "Ten Thousand Times Ten Thousand" "For All the Saints Who from Their Labors Rest" "When on My Day of Life the Night Is Falling" "Hark, Hark, My Soul, Angelic Songs Are Swelling" "Jerusalem, the Golden" "Heavenward Still Our Pathway Tends"

Acknowledgments

NUMEROUS leaders have supplied unpublished and original material for this volume, for which I am deeply grateful. Their contributions will be felt in the informal worship period of many Christian organizations and auxiliaries.

I am indebted for general guidance on the manuscript to Charles L. Wallis, an experienced anthologist, but naturally he is not to be held responsible for whatever shortcomings remain in the book.

For various valuable suggestions, I am grateful to Florence A. Partridge and Ruth Auchenbach of the Women's Guild of the Evangelical and Reformed Church, now merged in the United Church of Christ; Louise Auchenbach, a missionary from the Evangelical and Reformed Church to Japan; Mrs. W. M. Alexander, former Spiritual Life Secretary of the Woman's Division of Christian Service of the Methodist Church; Nevin E. Kendell, editor of the *Youth Fellowship Kit* published by The Westminster Press, who first asked me to contribute a number of organized devotional aids for that publication; Margaret B. Boies of the National Fellowship of Congregational Christian Women, now likewise merged in the United Church of Christ; John R. Scotford and William L. Leach for specific questions; and Mildred Smith of the Young Women's Christian Association of the United States of America.

Without the help of typists it would be difficult to imagine how the manuscript could have been prepared. I am indebted to Jocelyn Leibach for the first complete typing and to Rosalie M. Weiss for the typing of the second version and its partial revisions. I am also indebted to Miss Weiss for alphabetizing the sources and finishing the final forms.

Likewise I am deeply indebted to authors and publishers for supplying standard devotional aids. To those who own copyrights I wish to acknowledge indebtedness as follows:

Augsburg Publishing House: A prayer by Gertrude Doederlein in *Living with Our Children.*

Augustana Book Concern: A prayer from *God in Our Home* by Daniel Nystrom.

Donald Cameron: Hugh Cameron, *Prayers for Use in Public Worship.* Alexander Brunton.

The Christian Education Press: A prayer by Herbert W. Turner in *Prayer Book* by Karl H. A. Rest and a litany from *Epistle to White Christians* by Fred D. Wentzel.

Concordia Publishing House: A prayer from *Lutheran Book of Prayers* and a prayer by Elmer N. Witt in *Open the Meeting with Prayer* by Alfred Doerffler.

The Congregational Christian Churches in the United States, General Council: *A Book of Worship for Free Churches.* Oxford University Press.

Crown Publishers, Inc.: Martin Luther's prayer in *The Book of Prayers* edited by Leon and Elfrieda McCauley.

E. P. Dutton and Company: *Book of Common Worship,* edited by Wilbur P. Thirkfield and Oliver Huckel; a prayer by Archdeacon of Raphoe in *A Chain of Prayer Across the Ages* by Selina Fitzherbert Fox; John Hunter, *Devotional Services for Public Worship.*

Eden Publishing House: *Evangelical Catechism* and a prayer for April 25 from the March-April, 1957, issue of *Daily Talks with God.*

Evangelical and Reformed Church, General Council: *Book of Worship* (1947) and *The Book of Worship for the Reformed Church in the U.S.* (1926, originally by the Publication and Sunday School Board of the Reformed Church in the U.S.)

The First Congregational Church, Webster Groves, Mo.: A creed by Luther Kloss, May 20, 1900.

Friendship Press: A prayer of unknown origin, quoted as adapted in *Once There Were Two Churches* by Fred D. Wentzel.

Hallmark Cards, Inc.: Text of Christmas card 15 x 285-2.

Harper and Brothers: A prayer by John Wallace Suter in *Prayers of the Spirit* and a prayer by Frances Paget quoted in *Worship Resources for the Christian Year* edited by Charles L. Wallis.

Houghton Mifflin Company: A poem by James Russell Lowell in *Collected Works.*

Jackson, Son and Company: *Service Book and Ordinal of the Presbyterian Church of South Africa.*

William H. Leach, for a prayer by J. Richmond Morgan in the December, 1938, issue of *Church Management.*

Muhlenberg Press: Prayers by Marjory Louise Bracher in *Church School Prayers;* Leander M. Zimmerman, *Prayers for All People, for All Occasions.*

Mrs. Clarence L. Murdey, for a prayer in September, 1952, issue of *Guide Posts,* a publication of the Missions Council, Congregational Christian Churches.

National Council of Churches of Christ in the U.S.A., Division of Christian Education: Quotations from *The Revised Standard Version of the Holy Bible;* a prayer by Harold L. Ives in *Rural Life Prayers* published originally by the Commission on Worship; a prayer by Mark Rich in the September, 1954, issue of *Town and Country Church.*

Oxford University Press: *The Book of Common Prayer,* 1932 Revised Edition; *The Kingdom, the Power and the Glory,* an American Edition of *The Grey Book;* William E. Orchard, *The Order of the Divine Service for Public Worship.*

Pilgrim Press: *Book of Church Services,* Charles H. Richards, Chairman; Walter Rauschenbusch, *Prayers of the Social Awakening;* Florence M. Taylor in *Pilgrim-Primary Teacher,* April-June, 1950 issue.

The Presbyterian Church in Canada: *The Book of Common Order* of the Presbyterian Church in Canada, Second Revised Edition, Presbyterian Publications, Toronto.

The Presbyterian Church, U.S.A., Board of Christian Education: Louis F. Benson, *A Book of Family Worship; Social Progress,* February, 1949; *The Book of Common Worship,* 1946 Revised Edition.

Reformed Church in America, The Board of Publications: *The Liturgy of the Reformed Church in America.*

Charles Scribner's Sons: *Prayers for Services* by Morgan Phelps Noyes.

The United Lutheran Church in America: *Common Service Book of the Lutheran Church;* The United Lutheran Publishing House: John W. Doberstein, a prayer in *Prayers for Students.*

Charles L. Wan: *Book of Common Order of St. Giles' Cathedral.*

The Westminster Press: A poem by Harold C. Grunewald, prayers by F. Rest, and one adapted prayer from *The Book of Common Prayer* in *Worship Aids for 52 Services* by Friedrich Rest.

The Young Women's Christian Association of the U.S.A., National Board: Winnifred Wygal in *A Book of Prayers* by Helen Wright Mahon.

Sources

A LARGE proportion of the devotional aids appear in print here for the first time. The numbers in parentheses after the specific items refer to the sources. Where abridgments or adaptations of previously published prayers are made, the letters "ab" or "ad" are indicated within the parentheses as well.

1. *A Book of Worship for Free Churches.* Prepared under the direction of the Congregational Christian Churches in the U. S., General Council. Oxford University Press, 1948.
2. Allen, M. C.
3. Allrich, Fred C.
4. Archibald, W. S.
5. Auchenbach, Louise
6. Auchenbach, Ruth M.
7. Balliet Semmel, Irene
8. Benson, Louis F., *A Book of Family Worship.* Presbyterian Board of Publication, 1921.
9. Bergendoff, Conrad
10. Blackwelder, Oscar
11. Bode, D. A.
12. *Book of Church Services,* Pilgrim Press
13. *Book of Common Order of St. Giles' Cathedral.* Edinburgh, 1922.
14. *Book of Common Worship.* For use in the Several Communions of the Church of Christ. Wilbur Thirkfield and Oliver Huckel, editors. E. P. Dutton and Company, Inc., 1932.
15. *Book of Worship.* General Synod of the Evangelical and Reformed Church. Revised and Enlarged Edition. Central Publishing House, Cleveland, 1947.
16. Bracher, Marjory Louise, *Church School Prayers.* Muhlenberg Press, 1956.
17. Bright, William, *Ancient Collects.* James Parker and Company, Oxford and London. Compiled in 1875. Adapted.
18. Brokhoff, J. R.
19. Buehler, Bernice
20. Caldwell, Frank H.
21. Calvin, John
22. Cameron, Hugh, *Prayers for Use in Public Worship.* Alexander Brunton, Edinburgh, 1921.
23. Coleridge, Samuel T.

24. *Common Service Book of the Lutheran Church.* The General Synod of the Evangelical Lutheran Church in the U.S.A. The Trustees of the General Council of the Evangelical Lutheran Church in North America, and the United Synod of the Evangelical Lutheran Church in the South, 1917.

25. *Coptic Liturgy of St. Basil,* fourth century.

26. Damm, Henry J.

27. Doberstein, John W., in *Prayers for Students,* United Lutheran Publishing House.

28. Doederlein, Gertrude, in *Living with Our Children,* Augsburg Publishing House.

29. Eisenhower, Dwight D.

30. *Evangelical Book of Worship.* Published by the German Evangelical Synod of North America. Eden Publishing House, 1916. As adapted in *Worship Aids for 52 Services.*

31. *Evangelical Catechism.* Eden Publishing House, 1929, adapted originally from Luther's Small Catechism.

32. *Evangelical Catechism.* Evangelical Synod of North America. Eden Publishing House, 1929.

33. Fagerburg, Frank B.

34. Foelsch, Charles B.

35. Fox, Selina Fitzherbert, *A Chain of Prayer Across the Ages.* E. P. Dutton and Company, Inc., 1913. Prayer by Archdeacon of Raphoe.

36. Gillespie, George D., in John Wright's *Prayers for Priest and People,* Third Edition, Revised and Enlarged, The Young Churchman Company, 1908. Adapted.

37. Glover, Carl

38. *Gregorian Sacramentary,* A.D. 590.

39. Grunewald, Harold C., in Friedrich Rest's *Worship Aids for 52 Services.*

40. Haas, John R. C.

41. Haas, Manfred

42. Hallmark Cards, Inc., Text of Christmas card 15 x 285-2.

43. Herbster, Ben M.

44. Hershey, Robert D.

45. Hoefer, Elmer Henry

46. Homrighausen, E. G.

47. Horton, Douglas

48. Hunter, John, *Devotional Services for Public Worship.* E. P. Dutton and Company, Inc., J. M. Dent and Sons, Ltd., London. Ninth Edition, 1915.

49. Hunter, William M.

50. Irion, Paul E.

51. Ives, Harold L., *Rural Life Prayers,* Commission on Worship of the Federal Council of the Churches of Christ in America, Second Edition, revised, 1943.

52. Johansen, John H.

53. Kauffman, Constance Clapp

54. Keppel, A. R.

55. Kirkland, Bryant

56. Klemme, Huber

57. Statement of Faith approved by the Second General Synod of the United Church of Christ in July, 1959.

58. Knight, William Angus, *Prayers Ancient and Modern.* J. M. Dent and Sons, Ltd., London.
59. Koehler, B. J.
60. Kohler, J. Kenneth
61. Kostyu, Frank A.
62. Kuntzleman, W. A.
63. Langrebe, Karl U.
64. Leach, William H.
65. Lee, Henry W., in John Wright's *Prayers for Priest and People,* Third Edition, Revised and Enlarged, The Young Churchman Company, 1908.
66. *Liturgy of St. Chrysostom,* A.D. 398.
67. Lowell, James Russell, in *Collected Works.* Houghton Mifflin Company.
68. Loyola, Ignatius
69. *Lutheran Book of Prayers,* Concordia Publishing House.
70. Luther, Martin, as in McCauley, *The Book of Prayers,* Dell Publishing Company, Inc., 1954.
71. *Luther's Small Catechism.* First part of Question 207.
72. Lyons, Edward E.
73. Mackey, Sheldon E.
74. Martin, Florence B.
75. Martin, John, in *Intermediate Worship Programs*
76. Melanchthon, Philipp
77. Miller, L. C. T.
78. Miller, Martha
79. Morgan, J. Richmond, in *Church Management,* December, 1938, issue. Cleveland.
80. Morgan, J. Richmond, in Friedrich Rest's *Worship Aids for 52 Services.*
81. Murdey, Sarah, in September, 1952, issue of *Guide Posts,* Vol. 10, No. 3.
82. Nabers, Charles Haddon
83. National Board of the Young Women's Christian Association of the U.S.A.
84. Newman, John Henry
85. Niebuhr, Reinhold
86. Noyes, Morgan Phelps, *Prayers for Services.* Charles Scribner's Sons, 1934.
87. Nygaard, Norman E.
88. Nystrom, Daniel, *God in Our Home,* Augustana Book Concern, 1936.
89. O'Dell, A. Glen
90. Oldham, Dale
91. Doerffler, Alfred, *Open the Meeting with Prayer,* Concordia Publishing House, 1955. The prayer by Elmer N. Witt, based on the aims of the Walther League, is quoted because the aims of other groups could be similarly expressed.
92. Orchard, William E., *The Order of Divine Service for Public Worship.* Compiled from Ancient and Modern Devotions. Oxford University Press, London, 1921.
93. Oxenham, John
94. Paget, Francis, *Worship Resources for the Christian Year,* edited by Charles L. Wallis. Harper and Brothers, 1954.
95. Paine, R. Howard
96. Parker, Theodore
97. Pike, James A.
98. Poppe, Leona
99. Rauschenbusch, Walter, *Prayers of the Social Awakening.* The Pilgrim Press, 1909.

100. Reinartz, F. Eppling
101. Remmel, Marie Rose
102. Rest, Friedrich
103. Rest, Friedrich, in *Worship Aids for 52 Services*. Westminster Press, 1951.
104. Rest, Karl H. A.
105. Rest, Karl H. A., in *Daily Talks with God,* Eden Publishing House, April 25, 1957.
106. Rest, Paul
107. Rettig, Edna G.
108. Rich, Mark
109. Rich, Mark, in *Town and Country Church,* September, 1954.
110. Roggenkamp, Betty Jeanne
111. Sayres, Alfred N.
112. Scherzer, Carl J.
113. Schumacher, Theodore F.
114. Schweinfurth, Fred C.
115. *Service Book and Ordinal of the Presbyterian Church of South Africa.* Jackson, Son and Company, Glasgow, Second Edition, 1929.
116. Shinn, Roger L.
117. Snyder, Claude J.
118. *Social Progress,* February, 1949. The Board of Christian Education of the Presbyterian Church, U.S.A.
119. Stanger, R. C.
120. Suter, John Wallace, *Prayers of the Spirit.* Harper and Brothers, 1943.
121. Suter, John Wallace
122. Taylor, Florence M., in *Pilgrim-Primary Teacher,* April-June, 1950. Pilgrim Press.
123. Tiemeyer, T. N.
124. *The Book of Common Order.* Second Revised Edition, Presbyterian Publications, Toronto, 1948.
125. *The Hymnal.* Eden Publishing House, 1941.
126. *The Book of Common Prayer.* According to the Use of the Protestant Episcopal Church in the U.S.A. Revised Edition, Oxford University Press, 1932.
127. *The Book of Common Worship.* The Board of Christian Education of the Presbyterian Church in the U.S.A. Revised Edition, 1946.
128. *The Book of Worship for the Reformed Church in the U.S.* The Publication and Sunday School Board of the Reformed Church in the U.S., 1926.
129. *The Kingdom, the Power and the Glory.* An American Edition of *The Grey Book,* Oxford University Press, 1933.
130. *The Liturgy of the Reformed Church in America,* together with *The Psalter.* The Board of Publications of the Reformed Church in America, 1907.
131. Towle, Warren Wilder
132. Turner, Herbert W., in Karl H. A. Rest's *Prayer Book,* Christian Education Press, 1950.
133. Unknown Source. Adapted by Fred D. Wentzel in *Once There Were Two Churches.*
134. Unknown Source.
135. van Dyke, Henry
136. Vogel, Mrs. Willa Walters
137. Vogt, Von Ogden
138. Wagner, James E.
139. Wallis, Charles L.

140. Walters, Loren
141. Wentzel, Fred D., *Epistle to White Christians*, The Christian Education Press, 1948.
142. Wernecke, Herbert W.
143. Werner, Hazen
144. Wintermeyer, Herbert
145. Wobus, Paul A.
146. Wygal, Winnifred, in *A Book of Prayers*, by Helen Wright Ma-hon. National Board of the Young Women's Christian Association of the U.S.A.
147. National Board of the Young Women's Christian Association of the U.S.A.
148. Zimmann, William C.
149. Zimmerman, Leander, *Prayers for All People, for all Occasions*, Muhlenberg Press, 1939.

Bibliography

THE task of compiling additional material, especially that which is suited for the most widely observed days of the church year and the newer special days, calls for constant search and discrimination. Over a period of several years a small library of additional aids can be collected. Under the headings of poems, prayers, stories, and meditations are given here a list of suggested resources.

POEMS

Clark, Thomas Curtis. *Poems for Daily Needs*. Round Table Press, 1936.

Hill, Caroline M., ed. *World's Great Religious Poetry*. Macmillan, 1938.

Morrison, James Dalton, ed. *Masterpieces of Religious Verse*. Harper and Brothers, 1948.

PRAYERS

Bracher, Marjory Louise. *Church School Prayers*. Muhlenberg Press, 1956.

Collects and Prayers, Approved by the Joint Commission on the Liturgy and proposed for adoption by the cooperating churches. Muhlenberg Press, 1948.

Mahon, Helen Wright. *A Book of Prayers*. Publication Services, National Board of the Young Women's Christian Association of the U.S.A., 1952.

Merriam, Charles Wolcott. *Church Worship Book*. The Pilgrim Press, 1931.

Doerffler, Alfred. *Open the Meeting with Prayer*. Concordia Publishing House, 1955.

Rest, Friedrich. *Worship Aids for 52 Services*. Westminster Press, 1951.

Rest, Karl H. A. *Prayer Book*. The Christian Education Press, 1950.

Strodach, Paul Zellar. *Oremus—Collects, Devotions, Litanies from Ancient and Modern Sources*. Board of Publications of the United Lutheran Church in America, 1935.

The Kingdom, the Power and the Glory. An American edition of *The Grey Book*, Oxford University Press, 1933.

Wallis, Charles L., ed. *Worship Resources for the Christian Year*. Harper and Brothers, 1954.

Zimmerman, Leander M., *Prayers*. Muhlenberg Press, 1939.

STORIES AND MEDITATIONS

Applegarth, Margaret T. *Men As Trees Walking*. Harper and Brothers, 1952.

Cavert, Walter Dudley. *Story Sermons from Literature and Art*. Harper and Brothers, 1939.

Eggleston, Margaret W. *Forty Stories for the Church, School, and Home*. Harper and Brothers, 1939.

Morrill, Guy L. *Stewardship Stories*. Harper and Brothers, 1927.

Newton, Joseph Fort. *Everyday Religion*. Abingdon Press, 1950.

Niebuhr, Hulda. *Greatness Passing By*. Stories to Tell to Boys and Girls. Charles Scribner's Sons, 1931.

Rest, Karl H. A. *When Stones Hurt Your Feet*. Muhlenberg Press, 1954.

Scherzer, Carl J. *Followers of the Way*. The Christian Education Press, 1955.

Index

THE FOLLOWING INDEX refers to the numbers in front of the devotional aids throughout this book. Page numbers are given only for the material in chapter one.